the thing is

TONY PAYNE

The Thing Is
© Matthias Media 2013

Matthias Media
(St Matthias Press Ltd ACN 067 558 365)
Email: info@matthiasmedia.com.au
Internet: www.matthiasmedia.com.au
Please visit our website for current postal and telephone contact information.

Matthias Media (USA)
Email: sales@matthiasmedia.com
Internet: www.matthiasmedia.com
Please visit our website for current postal and telephone contact information.

ISBN 978 1 922206 42 8

Cover design and typesetting by Lankshear Design.

For Ian Carmichael, Emma Thornett, and all
the team at Matthias Media, whose long-term
fellowship, support and encouragement make
books like this possible.

1

The thing is.

That's what we say when we want to signal that the next words to come out of our mouths are (at last) the point. The bushes have been beaten around, the chase has been cut to, and we are finally getting to the 'thing'—to the issue we've been avoiding but that now needs to be spoken.

Perhaps it's your boss explaining why in fact you're not getting a pay rise; or your teenager owning up as to why you no longer have a side mirror on the car; or your boyfriend confessing the real reason he's breaking up with you.

In each case there is a slight pause, and sometimes an apologetic look for all the excuses and small talk that has led up to this, and then those three words: "The thing is". (Or if we're in America, "Here's the thing".)

Following those three words, and perhaps another brief silence, out comes the truth that we've been longing for or dreading. I can't give you a pay rise because you simply haven't been performing. I drove too close to a parked bus and took the mirror clean off. I just don't like being with you any more.

The 'thing' might be good news or bad. It might reassure us or shatter us. But at least now we have some clarity. We can stop pretending or avoiding the issue. We can strip back the layers and all the rubbish, and get to the reality that is there underneath, and which matters most.

We can talk about the thing that really is.

»

Imagine you're thrust into some new social setting—you've just joined a group at church, or you're attending a training course for work—and you're given five minutes to introduce yourself and give people a sense of who you are. You talk about what you do for a living, who your family are and where you grew up, what you like doing on the weekend, what your hopes for the future are, and so on. This goes on for a little while, but all of a sudden a wave of honesty sweeps over you and you pause, lean slightly forward, and say: "The thing is…"

What would come out of your mouth next?

If you had to spell out the thing that really makes sense of who you are, the basic truth that defines you, the real purpose or longing that drives you—what would it be?

I think most of us would find it a little hard to say, off the cuff. We don't tend to think about these big issues from week to week. And in one sense, we can't. We're too busy just surviving or getting on with whatever is dominating our life at the moment.

However, if we were forced to, or if we were given the time and space to, we all do have an answer to that question.

We all base our lives on something. We are all driven by something. In the midst of all the hassles and details of the daily grind, there are some basic truths that define us and give our lives meaning.

A college student in his early 20s might say, "The thing is: I just want to live for the moment. I hate all the expectations that people put on me. I just want to be me." A young mother in her early 30s might say, "The thing is: I've always dreamed of having a husband and children. But now that I have them, I'm not as happy as I thought I would be." A working man in his late 40s might say, "The thing is: I want to be a success, and do something that actually makes a difference. And I love my wife and kids. I just wish I could juggle it all better, because the truth is I feel pretty tired and worn down, and like I'm not really succeeding anywhere."

What would it be for you?

What is the often unspoken truth that really defines you? The longing that drives you? The 'thing' that really shapes who you are and what you do?

The aim of this short book is to help you answer those questions in a new way. It's a brief pause in the midst of our daily lives to explore the underlying truth about our daily lives. It's an opportunity to consider the 'thing' that we all must face at some point: *Who am I really, and does my life make any sense?*

Few questions are more significant. If there *is* some deeper meaning and purpose to our lives, what could be more important than knowing and understanding it, and living in its light? And what could be worse than living our entire lives without understanding what our lives were really for?

This in fact is one definition of freedom: to be and do what we were truly intended to be and do—like an old bat that has been used to prop open the laundry door, but is rescued and returns to the field of play to feel again the glorious freedom of striking the ball.

That's the freedom I want to write about in the chapters to follow.

»

I write these words as a Christian, and I expect that many of my readers will also be people of Christian conviction (although this book is not only for such people). For Christians, there are certain answers to these big questions that we know off by heart.

Who am I? As a Christian we might answer, "A child of God", or "A follower of Jesus Christ". And what is my purpose in life? Many Christians would say, "To give glory to God" or "To worship God in all that I do" or "To be a good Christian person".

However, in my experience these somewhat vague expressions don't always serve us well in the pressure and distraction of daily life. They are not sufficiently clear—or we have not clearly thought through what they mean. They certainly don't seem clear enough to *drive* our daily lives and make a difference to what we do, if the lives of many Christians are anything to go by.

For many of us, Christianity can feel like a veneer that has been tacked onto the surface of our lives. We go to church on Sundays. We might even do stuff at church on

Sundays, like hand out the bulletins or play in the band. And we have slightly higher (or different) moral standards to those around us. But in most other respects, our goals and aims in life seem indistinguishable from our neighbours. We want a nice house in a good street; we want to be secure and successful; we want to enjoy life and love; we want our kids to go to good schools and to turn out well; and so on.

The things that drive us and that really matter to us—our aspirations—don't seem to have been affected very much by what we say we believe when we stand up in church on Sundays—because they don't seem so different from the aspirations of all those people around us who aren't in church on Sundays.

My aim in what follows, then, is to challenge your understanding of the Christian faith and its answers to these big and basic questions. In particular, my hope is that you will gain:

- a fresh understanding of who God is, and what his purposes are in our world
- a fresh understanding of yourself—of who you really are, what you're here for, and what your future holds
- the clarity and freedom and joy of knowing what to do with the rest of your life from this point on.

Those are big aims for such a little book. But if the Bible and human history have taught us anything, it's that God has a habit of achieving great things through small, humble and outwardly unimpressive means. I pray that this book, which meets all three of these criteria, will be the unlikely means for God to do something extraordinary in your life.

2

28285633.

What does this eight-digit number mean?

As it happens, almost nothing. It's a sequence of digits I got from random.org, a website that will generate a string of random numbers of any length you require.

These eight numbers have no meaning and serve no real purpose. I could rearrange them and it wouldn't make the slightest difference to anyone. I could substitute some different numbers and no-one would care. There is no design or intention or conscious thought in these numbers. They just are.

The following eight numbers, however, are not random.
92334627.

These are the unique numbers assigned to the phone system at the Matthias Media office in Sydney where I work, and they mean something to me, to everyone who works at Matthias Media, and indeed to anyone who wants to call us. These numbers identify us, and they make communication with us possible. If I were to rearrange these numbers, or substitute some others, it really would matter.

These numbers are meaningful because they are the result of thought, design and intention. They are purposeful. And they share these characteristics of meaning and purpose with anything that is designed and made by someone.

We know this to be true—that for something to have meaning and purpose in its existence it must be the result of thought and design; it must be intended or planned. Purely random events and objects don't have meaning or purpose. In fact, that's what 'random' means in our language—that it just happened; it was accidental, unplanned and unintended. If someone looks at a random occurrence and asks, "Why did this happen? What was the meaning of this?", we sense that they're asking the wrong questions.

And so the big question is: What sort of thing is a human being? What sort of thing are you?

Are you a randomly generated number that has arisen through chance and accident, and is therefore without purpose or significance? Or are you a number that has been designed and created with intention and purpose?

As humans, we find it almost impossible to escape the sense that the latter is true. Even the most hardened atheist who insists that all life, including human life, is the result of undesigned, unplanned random occurrences over billions of years—even that atheist cannot bring himself to say that his life is purposeless, meaningless and of no significance.

And he will find it especially hard to say so in the face of evil. After the attacks of September 11, even the atheists started talking about 'evil' again. But in a random universe, 'evil' is a nonsensical word. We may experience an event as bad or unpleasant, but to give it a moral value—to call it 'evil'—is to admit that there is a meaning or purpose for human existence that is at this point being frustrated or destroyed. It is to admit that there is a 'should' to human life, a way that things ought to be; a way that things are *meant* to be.

The champions of a random, unplanned universe consisting purely of physical events and forces have no rational grounds for speaking in such a way, and yet they find themselves unable to stop doing so.

This is because the idea that human life is meaningful, valuable and purposeful resonates deeply within us. It makes sense of us and of our experience of life, in a way that the alternatives do not.

This leads us to the intuition that is also the first and foundational truth of Christianity: that Someone made us.

»

The opening pages of the Bible teach very clearly what we all know deep within ourselves to be true: that this is a created and meaningful world, not a random and accidental one. We learn that we humans did not come to exist by chance but by the purposeful action of a good and powerful creator, who gave meaning and purpose to his creation.

We see something of this purpose in the extraordinary account of the creation of the world in Genesis. In Genesis 1, God calmly and majestically speaks the world into existence. He creates the conditions and spaces for life (light, dark, air, water, land, sea) and then populates those spaces with plants and birds and fish and animals of every kind. At each point, God sees that what he has done is good.

Then we come to verse 26 of the chapter, and for the first time we hear God deliberating about what he is about to do and why. He says to himself,

> "Let us make man in our image, after our likeness. And
> let them have dominion over the fish of the sea and over
> the birds of the heavens and over the livestock and over
> all the earth and over every creeping thing that creeps on
> the earth." (Genesis 1:26)

God does here what all creators do. He approaches the creative act with a purpose in mind. In this case, the reason he creates humanity is so that they might occupy a place of "dominion" over the rest of his creation. No doubt this is one important reason he creates mankind as male and female—so that they might multiply and fill the earth, and take charge of it.

This is largely what is meant by humanity being made in the image of God. We are supposed to rule the world like God does, like a son in the family business. We may not have his infinite power (we cannot create a world by speaking it into existence!) but we are nevertheless like him in a way that the other creatures are not. They are all created "according to their kinds" (see Genesis 1:24-25), but we are made to be like God, to rule over the other creatures as he does, in goodness and wisdom.

Now we are only at page 1 of the Bible, and there is much still to be filled out and explained—such as what goodness and wisdom really are, not to mention why it is that our rule of the planet has been so catastrophic.

But even at this very early point in the Bible's story, some things are already stunningly clear. God is immensely powerful. He is the creator of everything that exists, and so he is its ruler and master. He is the one who fashions and orders his creation, and he is the one who gives purpose and meaning to it.

We, on the other hand, are creatures. We are manufactured. Like every other creature on the planet, we are the result of the thought, intention and action of God.

>>

These foundational ideas in Genesis are echoed and explained and developed throughout the sprawling biblical history that follows. And of all the passages that talk further about these ideas, none is more striking and shocking than the 45th chapter of the book of Isaiah.

Here's the situation: the twelve tribes of Israel are basically down to two (Judah and Benjamin). The other ten have been wiped off the map after a long history of wickedness, stubbornness and rebellion against God. And these last two—Judah and Benjamin—have also been defeated by the pagan Babylonians and carried off into exile, leaving their capital Jerusalem in ruins. Babylon, in turn, has been defeated by Persia, and the remnant of Israel is now in the hands of a new tyrant: the Persian King Cyrus, who is the undisputed ruler of the known world.

Israel is at its lowest ebb.

Into this bleak situation, God speaks through the prophet Isaiah and declares his intention to return the Israelites to their land. And what is more, he is going to use Cyrus the pagan king as his instrument to take them back and to rebuild the walls of Jerusalem.

In the words of the prophecy, addressed to Cyrus, God says:

> "I am the LORD, and there is no other,
> > besides me there is no God;
> > I equip you, though you do not know me,
> that people may know, from the rising of the sun
> > and from the west, that there is none besides me;
> > I am the LORD, and there is no other.
> I form light and create darkness,
> > I make well-being and create calamity,
> > I am the LORD, who does all these things." (Isaiah 45:5-7)

It is hard to imagine a more complete picture of God's supreme rule and power. He is in charge of everything—of light and darkness, of success and disaster, of the catastrophic destruction of Israel and also of their unlikely rehabilitation and return.

In fact, Israel cannot look anywhere else for an explanation of their plight in exile, because there is nowhere else to look. It's not as if there are other powerful gods who have bested Israel's God, resulting in Israel's defeat. No—your punishment and exile were my doing, says God, because there is no other god to blame. No matter how far east or west you search, there is just Me. I'm completely and totally in charge—including being able to direct and organize international leaders and events to achieve my purposes.

Cyrus may have been the most powerful man in the world at the time, but he is simply a pawn in God's hands. Cyrus may not know God, but God knows Cyrus, and will appoint him and equip him for the task that God has in mind for him—that is, to restore the Israelites to their land and city.

This is a bitter pill for Israel-in-exile to swallow. Imagine the Jews in the concentration camps of World War II, taken from their homes and shipped off into misery and suffering by a cruel and powerful Führer. Now imagine God saying to them that he was going to use Hitler as his appointed instrument to rescue the Jews and return them to their lands and homes. "Him?? You are going to use *him* as our rescuer and saviour?!? We don't want you to use him; we want you to DESTROY him!"

Such would have been the natural reaction of the captive Israelites to Isaiah's prophecy. Such too may be our natural reaction to the idea that God is in complete control of the world, and of our lives. If God is so supremely in control, we may wonder, why on earth is the earth the way it is? Why does he allow such evil to flourish? Why do some people suffer so terribly? Why does he not organize my life more to my liking?

However, God responds to this thought by reminding the Jewish exiles of the most basic of all truths. He points out that they are really in no position to argue:

> "Woe to him who strives with him who formed him,
>   a pot among earthen pots!
> Does the clay say to him who forms it, 'What are you
>   making?'
>   or 'Your work has no handles'?
> Woe to him who says to a father, 'What are you begetting?'
>   or to a woman, 'With what are you in labour?'"

Thus says the LORD,
    the Holy One of Israel, and the one who formed him:
"Ask me of things to come;

> will you command me concerning my children and
>> the work of my hands?
> I made the earth
>> and created man on it;
> it was my hands that stretched out the heavens,
>> and I commanded all their host.
> I have stirred [Cyrus] up in righteousness,
>> and I will make all his ways level;
> he shall build my city
>> and set my exiles free,
> not for price or reward,"
>> says the LORD of hosts. (Isaiah 45:9-13)

Israel is in no position to tell God what to do, or to dictate to him how he should make his plans. He is the Maker; they are the made. He made the earth and stretched out the heavens; they are the work of his hands. He is the potter; they are the clay. If God wishes to save Israel and rebuild Jerusalem by using a pagan king as his saviour, then that is precisely what he will do.

There is an inescapable truth here. If God is the creator and we are his creatures, then us telling God what to do is about as sensible as a coffee mug arguing with its potter. God is the creator and master of all—the great Potter who fashions and forms us, who decides what we are for and how he will use us. He is the one who determines what his creatures are for, and what they should do.

The thing is: *we* don't get to decide who we really are and what our lives are for—our creator does.

>>

Let's be honest. We hate this idea.

As we read the prophecy of Isaiah 45, we squirm at the thought that we are lumps of clay in the hands of our Potter, to do with as he pleases. We inwardly recoil at the suggestion that our priorities and dreams and goals in life should be determined for us by Someone Else. We deeply rebel against the notion that God should define who we are and tell us what to do.

It grates with everything we hold dear. A lifetime of Disney movies has taught us that you must be free to follow your heart, and that no-one else (least of all a Religious Authority Figure) can direct the course of your life. You must be yourself, and find the real truth about yourself within yourself. Only then can you believe in yourself, and be free to become your true self.

There are very few beliefs that everyone in Western society holds in common these days, but this is one of them: the absolute right to personal self-determination. When an external authority tries to impose its rules or priorities or values upon us, we protest (too loudly perhaps) that "*No-one* has the right to tell me how to live my life". In the words of the 60s anthem, "You gotta go where you wanna go, do what you wanna do, with whoever you wanna do it with…"[1]

There is a long history to the prominence of this idea in our world, and we do not have time to trace it here. But we do need to recognize how widespread it is in our culture. It is the air we breathe. It is the basic assumption

1   J Phillips, 'Go Where you Wanna Go', from the album *If You Can Believe Your Eyes*, Dunhill, Hollywood, 1966.

of every television show and movie we watch, every book we read, every song we hum along to. It's the bedrock of the education system that schooled us, and it's the common language of the social media space many of us now live and relate in.

It is the default position of all our minds, even of those of us who are Christians. We may know and acknowledge that God is truly God and that we should submit to *his* plans for our lives; yet we underestimate just how far down the roots of self-determination go in our souls. Ask any aging saint who has been a Christian for decades, and they will testify that the desire to rule our own lives runs very deep, and never leaves us.

The strange thing is, this deep attachment we have to self-determination contradicts the equally deep sense we have that human life is purposeful and meaningful. As we considered at the opening of this chapter, this idea that human life is purposeful resonates with all of us. We know at a visceral level that our lives are not meaningless or random. And yet this can only be the case if our lives are the result of design or intention—that is, if we came to exist not purely by the result of physical forces acting randomly, but through the intention and purpose of a creator.

And so we see the profound folly by which the human heart has always been bound. We sense very deeply that we have been made; that we were intended; that there is a purpose and meaning to human life that can only be the result of us being created by Another.

And yet we also stubbornly rebel against the idea that the purpose and direction of our lives can only be given to us by Another—that is, by the God who created us.

We want the freedom to live as if no-one created us, and yet we cannot abide the meaningless, purposeless nature of an accidental, non-created world.

All in all, we desire to be in the position of the potter rather than the clay.

And that desire, along with its tragic consequences, is as old as humanity itself.

3

If the truth about who we are and what our lives are for is given to us from outside—from the God who made us, and who rules over all—then the obvious and pressing question is: *What is that truth? Who am I really? What is my life really for?*

The rest of this book will seek to answer those questions, beginning in this chapter with another vital foundation.

We can't really grasp or understand what God's purpose for us is unless we clearly understand a very important fact about ourselves: we are not only creatures of God, formed by him like a potter with clay, but *we are creatures in rebellion against our Maker*. We belong to a rebel species who were created by God for a particular purpose but who from the very beginning rejected that purpose.

This rebellion against God and rejection of his agenda has massive implications. It changes the whole landscape. It not only affects each of us here and now every day, but (as we will see in coming chapters) also shapes the very nature of what God is now doing in the world, and how his purposes are being worked out.

In this chapter, then, we need to spend a little while digging around in the tragedy of the human situation. We need to explore the darkness and understand it, for if we do, we are more likely to recognize the light and run to it when we see it.

»

Most dramas start with an establishing scene. The camera pans across a peaceful garden to a cottage, and in through the kitchen window to a young family having breakfast together. Peaceful music plays in the background. Dad is getting ready for work. He engages in some friendly banter with his son at the table. His loving wife, who has everything under control, kisses him goodbye.

We know, of course, that very shortly all this is going to unravel. A tragedy will strike—a murder, an infidelity, an alien invasion. The music will become ominous. The idyllic picture will end up in pieces, and the rest of the story will be about trying to put it back together again.

The human drama is strangely similar. As we saw in our last chapter, Genesis begins with God creating a good and ordered world. He puts mankind within it, and it is clear that he has certain plans and purposes for his creation. It is a beautiful and idyllic picture, although not necessarily a finished picture. You don't get the sense in Genesis 1 and 2 that the story is over; that perfection and finality has been reached, and there is nothing more to unfold. The story is just beginning. God has told humanity to fill the earth and subdue it and have dominion over all its creatures. Humanity has a destiny and a purpose, and the story leaves us wondering how all that will work out.

But before anything much else happens, it all comes unstuck.

In Genesis 3, the serpent worms its way into the relationship between Eve and her creator. The woman listens to one of the crawling things over which she is supposed to have dominion, and comes to doubt God's intentions. Does God really have her best interests at heart, the serpent asks? Does he really want her to flourish, or is he trying to stop her reaching her potential?

Eve is persuaded, and decides to eat from the one tree that God has withheld from them. Her lunkhead of a husband, who is standing idly by while his wife does all the talking, obediently does the same.

The essence of their error is distrust in God's goodness, but it is also an unwillingness to recognize God's *God-ness*. Adam and Eve rebel against God's rule as God; they flout his clear commands; they wish to become like God themselves. They make a fateful play for control, for being able to chart their own purpose and destiny in life.

We know this story so well, not only because we may have heard it many times but also because we live it every day.

We begin to doubt whether God's ways really are in our best interests. We come to think that we know better, so we reach out and grasp the good and shiny thing in front of us, ignoring God's warnings and commands not to do so. This is the pride and folly of humanity—we see something bright and desirable before our eyes, something that is indeed pleasurable and good, and we grab it, refusing to concede that our creator might know better than we do what is really good about this particular thing and how it should be used.

Sex is the classic case. Take adultery, for example. People plunge into adultery because they find the good that is in it so attractive—romance, excitement, infatuation, sex. These are all indeed good things, created by a good God for our enjoyment. But in the wrong place at the wrong time in the wrong context, they have catastrophic consequences. Adultery is always destructive. It kills relationships, families and trust. It is easy to look at men and women who have committed adultery and wonder whether they ever did the maths: on one side of the equation, a short period of excitement and sexual pleasure; on the other side, years of heartache and regret, and the shattered lives of spouses and children. It doesn't add up.

Did Eve do the maths? Did the witless Adam who followed her? Did they stop to think that God remained God? Did they consider that an attempt to flout his commands and good purposes would not end well?

Apparently not. And so they are all judged, including the serpent, and they face the consequences.

The punishment they receive is just and dreadful. It not only brings death and decay into their lives, but strikes at the heart of their purpose in the world—of being fruitful and multiplying and subduing the earth:

To the woman he said,

"I will surely multiply your pain in childbearing;
    in pain you shall bring forth children.
Your desire shall be for your husband,
    and he shall rule over you."

And to Adam he said,

> "Because you have listened to the voice of your wife
>   and have eaten of the tree
> of which I commanded you,
>   'You shall not eat of it,'
> cursed is the ground because of you;
>   in pain you shall eat of it all the days of your life;
> thorns and thistles it shall bring forth for you;
>   and you shall eat the plants of the field.
> By the sweat of your face
>   you shall eat bread,
> till you return to the ground,
>   for out of it you were taken;
> for you are dust,
>   and to dust you shall return." (Genesis 3:16-19)

Childbirth becomes painful; conflict enters the marriage relationship; even the very ground itself becomes unyielding and hostile. Rather than working the ground and making something of it, Adam will struggle against it until he himself returns to the ground in death.

This is the world we still live in—a world marred by death and decay, by conflict with each other, by struggle, pain, suffering and difficulty; a world where humanity seems able to do and achieve so much that is good, but in the next breath to do and achieve so much that is evil.

In Genesis we see it all in outline. We see the basic problem: humanity's stupid rebellion against our creator and God. We also see the basic consequences: death and decay, suffering and pain, conflict and hardship.

All this has obvious implications for our lives; for understanding what we are like, what we are for, and where we are headed. For a start, and most obviously, it means that our lives will come to an end. Whatever plans or dreams we construct for ourselves, we have no control over whether we will be around tomorrow to pursue them. We will return to dust, and all the dreams and hopes we might have had will dissolve into dust with us.

It also means that the road we tread between birth and death will be a difficult one in our relationships and in our work. The course of our lives won't be a smooth path of rose petals and sunshine. It will be rocky, painful, frustrating and difficult.

All this is foreshadowed and outlined in Genesis 1-3. And as the revelation of the Bible unfolds, this outline is filled out. We see more clearly and in more detail the nature of our sinfulness and rebellion, the nature of the consequences, and what it means for our daily lives and for our future.

We see all of this no more clearly than in the rather depressing biblical book of Ecclesiastes.

>>

During the folk revival of the 1960s, Pete Seeger set the first 8 verses of Ecclesiastes 3 to music and came up with what can only be described as an unlikely hit:

To everything, turn, turn, turn,
There is a season, turn, turn, turn,
And a time for every purpose under heaven,
A time to be born, a time to die…[2]

2   P Seeger, 'Turn! Turn! Turn! (To Everything There is a Season)', from the album *Turn! Turn! Turn!*, Columbia, Hollywood, 1965.

Seeger's version of Ecclesiastes 3 is in many ways an optimistic song. He sings not of "a time for war, and a time for peace" (as Ecclesiastes does), but simply of "a time for peace, I swear it's not too late".

In the context of the 60s and the peace movement and the Vietnam War, this was a powerful message of hope. Just give peace a chance; it's easy if you try. Imagine all the people, sharing all the world.

But this message of peace and love is not really the message of Ecclesiastes 3, which is at the same time a sadder and more realistic portrait of the world we live in. The author of Ecclesiastes often dwells on the frustrating pointlessness of our lives. The sun rises and falls; a generation is born and dies, only to be followed by another that also dies; nothing is ever really achieved; it all dissipates and is forgotten; the world just seems to go round and round and never get anywhere; there is nothing new under the sun; it is all vanity and wind.

Ecclesiastes 3 builds on this picture of pointlessness by considering the different experiences of our human life. There is a time for everything, and its opposite. Sometimes we plant; sometimes we pluck up what is planted. Sometimes we weep; sometimes we laugh. Sometimes we mourn; sometimes we dance. There is even a time for war, just as there is a time for peace.

Everything seems to have its time, and to fit in its time. In fact, in verse 11, the writer says that God "has made everything beautiful in its time". And we can sense that this is true—that there is a God at work in our world, who lives in eternity, and who gives meaning and significance to human life. We know that there is a larger purpose, a larger framework, in which the things that happen in the world make at least some kind of sense.

This is what the author means by saying that God "has put eternity into man's heart" (verse 11). We know there is more to life than just one thing happening randomly after another. We know there is a larger reality that explains our world, and gives some meaning and sense to what happens in it—such that we keep recognizing beauty and rightness and goodness in the various events and activities of our lives.

And yet… even though we know there is a God at work in our world, we "cannot find out what God has done from the beginning to the end", as the writer says (verse 11). We cannot figure out God's purposes and actions. We sense there is purpose and meaning to our lives—or that there should be—but it eludes us.

We experience this all the time—the frustration of just not knowing why something is happening, or where it's going, or what the overall purpose is. Life is opaque to us. It's not a window we can look through to see the big picture on the other side. It's frosted glass. We know there is something on the other side. We see the shadows moving, but we can't figure out what it is.

All this is very frustrating and humbling. What the writer goes on to say in Ecclesiastes 3 only intensifies this feeling:

> Moreover, I saw under the sun that in the place of
> justice, even there was wickedness, and in the place of
> righteousness, even there was wickedness. I said in my
> heart, God will judge the righteous and the wicked, for

there is a time for every matter and for every work. I said
in my heart with regard to the children of man that God
is testing them that they may see that they themselves
are but beasts. For what happens to the children of man
and what happens to the beasts is the same; as one dies,
so dies the other. They all have the same breath, and man
has no advantage over the beasts, for all is vanity. All go
to one place. All are from the dust, and to dust all return.
(Ecclesiastes 3:16-20)

The writer takes us back to the garden, where man and
beast are both formed from the dust of the earth, and have
God's breath breathed into their nostrils. He reminds us of
the awful judgement that has fallen on humanity. We have
been cast out of the garden and denied any further access to
the tree of life that stood at its centre. So now we must die
and return to the dust, just like the beasts.

Death is the one terrible fate that awaits all creatures. And
it pricks the bubble of human pride and self-importance.
We make such grand plans, we think we will achieve such
great things, but death stalks us and will have us we know
not when; and in the face of death, all our plans and dreams
are about as significant as the plans and dreams of a cow.

The apostle James says much the same thing in the New
Testament:

Come now, you who say, "Today or tomorrow we will go
into such and such a town and spend a year there and
trade and make a profit"—yet you do not know what
tomorrow will bring. What is your life? For you are a mist
that appears for a little time and then vanishes. Instead
you ought to say, "If the Lord wills, we will live and do

this or that." As it is, you boast in your arrogance. All such boasting is evil. (James 4:13-16)

We need to feel the weight of this if we are going to understand our lives and where they are going. We need to face honestly just how fickle, frustrating and fragile human life can be outside of Eden. We need to repent of the foolish dream that we can actually control our lives, and bend the world to our will. We can't. Some of us know this already from bitter experience. Some of us might still be living the fantasy that we are in control, and that we can chart our own destiny and make all our dreams come true. But we can't.

This is the other side of the conclusion we came to in our previous chapter. It's not only that God as our creator should define who we are and what our lives are for; *it's that on our own we are completely incapable of doing so*. We experience moments of beauty and goodness and rightness; we see hints of purpose and meaning. And yet life is also opaque to us. We can't figure out the bigger picture, nor discover what our lives are really about. We don't have the knowledge and the perspective to be able to craft an agenda for our lives that really makes sense. And even when we try, the fickleness and unpredictability of the world frustrate our plans.

But it's even worse than that. It's not only that the world is frustrating and unpredictable, and that we cannot control or master it. It's not only that death shatters all our grand dreams. There is also the constant reality of wickedness and evil. As the author says in the passage above: "Moreover, I saw under the sun that in the place of justice, even there was wickedness, and in the place of righteousness, even there was wickedness" (verse 16).

We are not simply innocent victims trapped by an unfortunate series of events. We are active and malevolent participators in the whole corrupt pantomime. Injustice and evil and wickedness penetrate everywhere—even to the very institutions that are supposed to uphold and protect justice and righteousness. And what is true of society as a whole is true also in our own daily lives and relationships. We like to think that we are basically honest and would do the decent thing; but when our own plans or desires are being thwarted, we are only too ready to lie, cheat, steal, manipulate and do whatever damage to others is necessary in order to get what we want.

So it's not just that we are limited and ignorant in our ability to shape our own lives, and that our grand plans are shadowed by death. We also actively compete with and sabotage one another in a frustrated and ultimately futile attempt to get our own way, build our own success, and fulfil our own purposes.

No wonder the author of Ecclesiastes shakes his head and utters his constant judgement on human life and striving: vanity, vanity, all is vanity. It's all empty; it's all temporary; it's all like a breath of wind that kisses your cheek and is gone.

Sometimes bad news is actually good news—such as when you've had a nagging health problem that has dragged on for months, and the doctor finally figures out what's wrong with you. Even though it's bad news (you've got a particular disease), in another sense it's good news because at least now you can start treating the problem.

The dismal conclusions we have now reached are like that.

The sin of humanity, and God's judgement on it, seem to have derailed God's good purposes for his world. Death and decay are now universal, injustice and wickedness are everywhere, and bad things happen to people seemingly without rhyme or reason. All in all we don't really know where we're going, what life is about, or what it is that really distinguishes us from the beasts, since—like them—we will return to dust, and all of our dreams and achievements will likewise turn to dust.

In the face of this dire and frustrating situation, the best we can do is enjoy the moment, if we happen to be blessed with that possibility.

This vision of life from Ecclesiastes is very like the vision that most of our neighbours and friends share: that is, there are good things in life worth enjoying (food, work, family, leisure, and so on). But life is also so chaotic, unpredictable and (often) awful, that there is no point trying to come up with a grand scheme or design. We don't really know what God is like or what life is about, so we might as well live for the moment, or the few moments ahead.

But, as the writer of Ecclesiastes points out, this makes us little different from the beasts, who also live for the next mouthful of grass they will chew, and like us return to the dust when they die.

Now if the story stops here, it would be like the doctor giving us the bad news, "You have a very serious illness", and then saying, "And by the way, there is no cure".

But thanks be to God, the story doesn't stop there. The

whole Bible is the story of God's answer to the problem, if we can put it like that.

And his answer is not just information: that is like the answer to a riddle. His answer is also an action, like the answer to a disease (which is a cure).

In fact, as we will begin to see in the chapters to follow, God's answer is even more than information and even more than an action. It is a person.

4

We have come far enough in our journey to pause and look back over the road behind us.

We started by talking about the big questions of our lives that we often don't get around to confronting and clarifying, particularly: *What is the meaning and purpose of my life?*

We started by seeing that God defines who we really are and what the purpose of our lives are—because our fundamental relationship with him is as creature to creator. He gets to decide what our lives are for, because he made us. He is the potter; we are the clay. The idea that we should determine our own meaning and purpose in life is rather absurd—like the clay deciding its own destiny in defiance of the potter.

But we saw in chapter 3 that this is precisely what we do. We don't like God being in charge of our lives, even though he has every right to be. We're like a certain kind of rebellious teenager, who lives her life in a self-obsessed bubble and regards her parents as inconveniences who should leave her alone to do as she pleases.

We also explored the consequences of humanity's rebellion against our creator: we suffer God's rightful judgement against us, and our lives are thus marred by difficulty, injustice, pain and death. In particular, we are afflicted with a frustrating inability to understand the bigger picture or story of what is happening in our lives. Although we do glimpse meaning and goodness in our world and our daily lives, we are unable to see beyond this to understand what it is all for and where it is all going. In fact, from where we sit, life often seems confusing, incomprehensible and just wrong.

This renders us incapable of working out our own purpose or agenda for life, let alone one that we can actually fulfil. (Doesn't stop us trying, of course.)

The point we have come to is this: *God not only has the right to say who we are and to determine the purpose of our lives; but he alone is able to do so, because he alone knows what the world and our lives are really for.*

Which leaves us with the crucial question: What are our lives really for? What purpose does God have for the world he has made?

>>

Many passages in the Bible reveal or summarize God's great purpose for our world and for our lives. The one that we are going to delve into is part of a letter written by the apostle Paul to some Christians in a little town called Colossae, in what is now Turkey. He had never met them personally, although his friend Epaphras was from Colossae and had been the one to preach the Christian message there.

Paul writes to these Colossian Christians to teach them more about the message they had heard and responded to, and to encourage them to stick with it. Early in the letter, he points out that they are not the only ones who had heard this profound message (or 'gospel'). In fact, it was spreading all over the world:

> Of this you have heard before in the word of the truth, the gospel, which has come to you, as indeed in the whole world it is bearing fruit and increasing—as it also does among you, since the day you heard it and understood the grace of God in truth, just as you learned it from Epaphras our beloved fellow servant. (Colossians 1:5-7)

This momentous message was spreading everywhere, like the passionfruit vine that used to grow on our back fence when I was growing up. The vine would insinuate its way along the fence, sending out tendrils, gaining a foothold on a new fence post, pushing out leaves, and bearing fruit at each point. We never noticed the spread of the vine; just that it was further along the fence every year. I can still smell and taste the vivid flesh of the passionfruit, picked fresh, split in half and mixed with some ice cream or fruit salad.

The spread of the gospel was like that: growing, spreading and making its way in the world, not by military takeover or with political fanfare but by the simple spreading of a vivid message that bore fruit in people's lives; that completely changed their lives.

What was this fruit in the lives of the Colossians? Paul gets to the heart of it later in the passage when he says:

> He has delivered us from the domain of darkness and transferred us to the kingdom of his beloved Son, in whom we have redemption, the forgiveness of sins. (Colossians 1:13-14)

The 'he' in this passage is God himself. Through the speaking and spreading of the gospel message, God had done something radical in the lives of the Colossians (and in the lives of Paul and Epaphras and all the rest). God had changed where they live. He had *delivered* or rescued them from the domain of darkness, and *transferred* them to the kingdom of his Son.

It was essentially a migration program. God was rescuing people from one realm or domain or country and transferring them to another—from a domain shrouded in darkness to one bathed in light.

What does Paul mean by "the domain of darkness"? It's a vivid image of the dismal situation we explored in the previous chapter. As a consequence of rebelling against God and his rule, humanity has been shut out from God and the light of his presence. We defiantly set our own plans for our lives, but we find ourselves seeking to achieve them in a dark realm ruled by decay and difficulty and death. It is a land we can never escape from, a land in which we are prisoners of our own independence.

As citizens of this domain we all have one thing in common: we oppose God. Some of us oppose him in a passive-aggressive sort of way, others in a more defiantly rebellious way. But we are all "alienated and hostile" in our minds, as Paul puts it in verse 21 of the chapter.

Tragically, this is home for us. It's where we live, trapped in a darkness that has become so normal for us that we hardly notice it any more.

This is why the gospel message is so powerful and revolutionary. It declares that God has undertaken a rescue mission to free those living in the realm of darkness, and to take them to a new land, a new kingdom: the kingdom of his Son.

We'll think more below about what it means to now live 'in the kingdom of his Son', but we first need to notice how the deliverance takes place. How is this 'transfer' achieved?

It is by another transfer of a different kind. Our guilt and sin and rebellion, and the punishment that was due, have been transferred to Jesus, who bore them all on the cross. As Paul says later in our passage:

> For in him all the fullness of God was pleased to dwell, and through him to reconcile to himself all things, whether on earth or in heaven, making peace by the blood of his cross. And you, who once were alienated and hostile in mind, doing evil deeds, he has now reconciled in his body of flesh by his death, in order to present you holy and blameless and above reproach before him...
> (Colossians 1:19-22)

Where there was alienation there is now reconciliation. Where there was evil, there is now blamelessness. Where there was hostility there is now peace.

All this God did through the blood of the cross, and we can scarcely believe why. We were, after all, the ones at fault—like rebellious little clay pots shaking our collective fists at the Potter, running away from home, refusing to live under his rule, building our own towers of Babel in his face.

And yet God, being rich in mercy, because of the great love with which he loved us, even when we were dead in our sins, made us alive together with Christ—as Paul puts it elsewhere (Ephesians 2:4-5).

It is astounding, and worthy of much more exploration than we will give it here (we will return to the subject in our next chapter).

The thing to notice at this point is that, according to Paul's letter, *this is God's great purpose in the world.* He is rescuing people (like the Colossians) from the domain of darkness and migrating them to the kingdom of his Son. As the gospel message of the cross spreads to every corner of the world, and as people hear and understand "the grace of God in truth" (as Paul calls it in 1:6), the great transfer takes place. Sins and guilt and punishment are transferred from us to Jesus, and we are transferred out of the domain of darkness and into his light-filled kingdom.

Paul says later in chapter 1 of Colossians that this was always God's plan, although it was kept secret for the longest time. It was a "mystery kept hidden for ages and generations but now revealed to his saints. To them God chose to make known how great among the Gentiles are the riches of the glory of this mystery, which is Christ in you, the hope of glory" (Colossians 1:26-27).

This is God's priority and purpose in the world, even now. Like a passionfruit vine spreading its way down the fence line of history, the fruit of his Passion has continued to grow in people's lives, right down to today—to Sydney in Australia where I am writing this, and to wherever it is that you are reading these words. Everywhere the gospel message has gone, it has been the means of God transferring rebels out of the domain of darkness and into the kingdom of his Son.

But that, as the infomercial always says, is not all.

>>

I have never migrated from one country to another. The farthest I have ever moved was 500 miles from our family farm to go to university in Sydney. It was more than 30 years ago, but I can still remember the swirling sense of excitement, anxiety and disorientation of those early months in the Big Smoke. New streets, new transport, new housemates, new church… new everything.

Needless to say, university was also a new experience. The very first day I turned up to class, the Marxist-nihilists (or was it the Leninist-feminists?) had called a student strike against the fascists who were apparently running the faculty. Placards were waved. Things were thrown. Angry speeches were given denouncing the corruption of the regime. And there was me, wide-eyed in my flannelette shirt and desert boots, foolscap notepad under my arm, wondering whether I was supposed to be getting any of this down.

Eventually, I did what most country kids do. I adapted, learned the lingo, traded in the flannelette shirt for a very fetching turtleneck, and began to live the Sydney student life.

In a vastly more profound change of address, God has moved us from one domain to another, from one ruler to another, from one life to another. And as is very clear from the opening chapter of Colossians, this initial transfer is just the beginning of the changes in our lives. Like any immigrant, we need to adjust to a whole new culture, marked not by hostility towards God but by a glad and grateful desire to please him. Paul prays for the Colossians that this new life would continue and grow in them:

> And so, from the day we heard, we have not ceased
> to pray for you, asking that you may be filled with
> the knowledge of his will in all spiritual wisdom and
> understanding, so as to walk in a manner worthy of the
> Lord, fully pleasing to him, bearing fruit in every good
> work and increasing in the knowledge of God. May you
> be strengthened with all power, according to his glorious
> might, for all endurance and patience with joy, giving
> thanks to the Father, who has qualified you to share in
> the inheritance of the saints in light. (Colossians 1:9-12)

It's clear that God's purpose for the Colossians (and for us) is not just to transfer them out of darkness and into his Son's kingdom, but to see their lives *transformed* as they live in that new kingdom. That is certainly what Paul prays that God would do for them—fill their minds with a new spiritual wisdom, fill their lives with a new God-pleasing fruitfulness, fill their souls with a new endurance and joy and thankfulness.

To *transfer* rebels out of darkness and to *transform* them in the kingdom of his Son—this would be a neat summary from Colossians 1 of what God is doing in the world; what his plan and purpose is; what his agenda is.

Except that we have missed out something vital.

»

From what we have said so far, it sounds like *we* are at the top of God's agenda. His plans, after all, revolve around us: rescuing us, forgiving us, reconciling us, transferring us, transforming us.

Perhaps we are right to think of ourselves like a very spoiled teenager. Maybe God's world does revolve around us. Maybe God is like an overly invested parent who lives entirely through his children, and who has no other purpose in life except to look after us and see us thrive. Maybe *we* are the reason God gets out of bed in the morning.

Many people today, including some Christians, think this is what Christianity really is—the conviction that God exists for our sake, to bless us, to save us, to make our lives better, and to help us to reach our potential.

But the section of Colossians 1 that we haven't yet looked at tells a different story. There's a bigger reason, a bigger item that dominates God's plans—in fact, one single item, of which everything else is a sub-point.

It concerns his Son:

> He is the image of the invisible God, the firstborn of all creation. For by him all things were created, in heaven and on earth, visible and invisible, whether thrones or dominions or rulers or authorities—all things were created through him and for him. And he is before all things, and in him all things hold together. And he is the head of the body, the church. He is the beginning, the firstborn from the dead, that in everything he might be preeminent. (Colossians 1:15-18)

God's highest purpose is to crown his Son Jesus as the Lord and Ruler of all. His plan has always been to enthrone Jesus as the crucified and risen Saviour King, who purchased a people for himself from every tribe and nation—including Colossians, Americans, Scandinavians, Peruvians and even Australians. His extraordinary purpose, his overriding goal and aim, is to exalt the name of his crucified and risen Son far above every other name that can be named, and for every knee to bow and every tongue to confess that Jesus Christ is Lord, to the glory of God the Father (as he puts it in Philippians 2:9-11).

This may be uncomfortable news for us, but we are not the centre of the universe; nor are we the reason that God made the world. As Colossians reminds us, "all things were created through him and *for him*"—that is, for the Son. The gospel announcement is about *him*, not us. It's that we can be saved *by him*, that we can be transferred into *his kingdom*, that we can be transformed to be *like him*.

There is really only one item on God's list, one purpose, one priority—if we can put it like that. It's the rule and glory of his Son. And the utterly extraordinary truth is that people like you and me can be part of that. God is gathering people like you and me and including us in his cosmic purpose to make Jesus Christ the king of a new kingdom of transferred and transformed people.

This requires a revolution in our thinking. It turns our world upside down, and changes our whole vision of reality.

It's like Neo swallowing the blue pill and becoming aware for the first time that his whole life has been 'lived' within a false computer-generated matrix.

It's like Copernicus realizing that the earth orbits the sun, and not the other way around.

The Son is indeed the centre of the universe that God has created, and God's purpose is to populate his kingdom with forgiven transformed rebels—like you and me.

When this truth dawns on us, and we appreciate its

magnitude, our lives can never be the same again. We discover who we truly are, and what our lives are really for.

5

In our last chapter, we penetrated to the very heart of the Christian message—the gospel that Epaphras preached to the Colossians, and that Paul and the other apostles preached around the ancient world, and that has spread all over the world and come even to us, as to those untimely born. We saw that the message was about a great transfer—of our sins onto Jesus, and of us out of the domain of darkness— and that this was the result of God's extraordinary plan to populate the kingdom of his Son.

But this 'word of truth' that Paul preached raised a question in people's minds back then that has also been asked ever since: if God has freely and completely forgiven us through the death and resurrection of Jesus, and transferred us into his kingdom, then *what incentive is there for us to lead a different life*? If I slip up, won't I be forgiven anyway? So does it really make any great difference how I live—as long as I avoid doing anything grossly immoral (like adultery)?

In my experience, very few Christians would be as crass as to put the question like this (at least aloud). But we do often struggle to understand how and why the cross of Jesus should make a real practical difference in our daily lives. We can feel that the cross is big and cosmic and 'spiritual'; and yet our lives are a daily grind of mundane details and tasks and responsibilities. God may have a massive plan focused on his Son, but at times that feels far removed from me and my everyday life.

Just how does God's grand purpose in Christ connect with us, and make a *difference* in our lives? How does it define who we are? How does it motivate and change us?

To answer that question, we are going to venture into one of the most profound sentences in all of human literature.

>>

Was the apostle Paul the teeniest bit nuts?

The Christians at Corinth evidently thought so, and on reasonable grounds. Paul lived in a way that most sane, ordinary folk would regard as unbalanced, unhealthy and possibly unhinged.

For example, in seeking to prove his authority and credentials as an apostle, Paul provides the following list of accomplishments:

> But whatever anyone else dares to boast of—I am speaking as a fool—I also dare to boast of that. Are they Hebrews? So am I. Are they Israelites? So am I. Are they offspring of Abraham? So am I. Are they servants of Christ? I am a better one—I am talking like a madman—with far greater labours, far more imprisonments, with countless beatings, and often near death. Five times I received at the hands of the Jews the forty lashes less one.

Three times I was beaten with rods. Once I was stoned.
Three times I was shipwrecked; a night and a day I was
adrift at sea; on frequent journeys, in danger from rivers,
danger from robbers, danger from my own people,
danger from Gentiles, danger in the city, danger in the
wilderness, danger at sea, danger from false brothers;
in toil and hardship, through many a sleepless night,
in hunger and thirst, often without food, in cold and
exposure. And, apart from other things, there is the daily
pressure on me of my anxiety for all the churches. Who is
weak, and I am not weak? Who is made to fall, and I am
not indignant? (2 Corinthians 11:21-29)

What sort of CV is this? It's certainly not the lifestyle of
a normal person. It's the behaviour of an extremist and a
fanatic. This was evidently what the Corinthian Christians
were thinking. Was Paul really a genuine apostle and man
of God? Do truly 'spiritual' people behave in this excessive,
almost lunatic, fashion?

In chapter 5 of his second letter to them, Paul opens his
heart and mind to the Corinthians and explains what drives
him to live the way he does. In the end, he says, it's because
he has no choice. The "love of Christ controls us" he says
(v. 14). Christ's love compels him, hems him in, and provides
him with no option but to live a completely different life.

What does he mean by this? In what way does the love
of Christ compel Paul's actions?

One thing he *doesn't* mean is that Christ's love motivates
him merely by way of inspiration or example. It is certainly
true that Christ's sacrifice on the cross is an example—
perhaps the ultimate example—of selfless love and sacrifice

for the sake of others. And there are places in the New Testament where his example is held up for Christians to follow (e.g. 1 Peter 2:20-21).

But here Paul is talking about something far more profound, and he explains it by penning one of the most remarkable sentences ever written:

> For the love of Christ controls us, because we have concluded this: that one has died for all, therefore all have died; and he died for all, that those who live might no longer live for themselves but for him who for their sake died and was raised. (2 Corinthians 5:14-15)

Christ's love controls or compels Paul because he is convinced of a certain truth: *that one died for all.*

This is not particularly difficult to understand or grasp. In fact, one man dying instead of or on behalf of others is a very familiar idea to us. It's a staple image of Western literature and film.

For a high culture example, it would be hard to go past the gripping climax of Charles Dickens's *A Tale of Two Cities,* in which the no-good Sydney Carton does the only decent thing he's ever done in his life by stepping in to be executed in the place of his close friend (and look-alike) Charles Darnay. He dies as a substitute for his friend, uttering the immortal words: "It is a far, far better thing that I do, than I have ever done; it is a far, far better rest that I go to than I have ever known."

For a pop culture example, consider *Deep Impact*, the B-grade disaster epic about a giant asteroid on a catastrophic collision course with Earth. Morgan Freeman as President dispatches a band of brave astronauts in their ship, *The Messiah* (get it?!), to save the world. Somewhat predictably, after many setbacks they fulfil their mission by selflessly flying their ship into the heart of the asteroid and blowing it (and themselves) to smithereens.

There are many, many stories like this in our cultural library. (You can search sermonillustrations.com for a ton of them.)

And this indeed is very like what Jesus did on the cross. According to Scripture, when Jesus died it was as our substitute, taking the full force of God's anger upon himself in the place of guilty sinners. "He himself bore our sins in his body on the tree," says 1 Peter 2:24, "that we might die to sin and live to righteousness." Or in the haunting words of Isaiah, so many centuries before Christ's death:

> He was pierced for our transgressions;
> > he was crushed for our iniquities;
> upon him was the chastisement that brought us peace,
> > and with his wounds we are healed. (Isa 53:5)

If you have any knowledge of the Christian gospel at all, this will be familiar ground to you—holy and familiar ground. We take our stand on that ground, and sing for joy:

> Bearing shame, and scoffing rude
> In my place, condemned, he stood
> Sealed my pardon with his blood
> Hallelujah, what a Saviour![3]

---

3   P Bliss, 'Hallelujah! What a Saviour', 1875.

However, as magnificent and true as these ideas are, it's not quite what Paul is saying here in 2 Corinthians 5. We need to press further to understand why Christ's love on the cross compels him.

You see, the logical conclusion Paul draws from the death of Christ is not the one we would draw as we think about Christ as our substitute. We might finish Paul's sentence this way: "one has died for all… so that all do not have to die; he has paid the wages of sin on our behalf, so that we might escape the sentence of death and have eternal life". But this is not what Paul says. He reaches a different conclusion. He says, "one has died for all, *therefore all have died*".

This takes some absorbing. It's not that Christ died so that I wouldn't have to die. On the contrary, says Paul. Christ died so that I *would* die. The result of Christ's death was my death. He died for all, and therefore all died.

In other words, Christ not only died as a substitute; he also died as a *representative*. He died *as* me, so that his death was also mine.

We are familiar with the idea of representation from politics. When we elect someone to parliament or congress, they go as our representative. They don't vote in parliament *instead* of us, as if it were a case of either them or us voting. They vote *for* us, as our representative, so that their vote counts as our vote. This means that in affairs of state, the former tennis professional who is now my local member of parliament acts *for* me and for everyone else in his electorate. He is (alas) our representative. And all we have to do in order to have his vote count as our vote in government is to live in his electorate.

What this means is that Christ did not only die instead of us; he also died our death *for* us, as our representative. When he died, we also died—provided of course that he is our representative, and that we live in his electorate.

'Living in Christ's electorate' is another way of describing what we saw in our last chapter—of being transferred by God out of the domain of darkness and into the kingdom of his Son. From our side, this means ceasing our stupid rebellion against God and giving all our trust, loyalty and obedience to the king of God's new kingdom, Jesus Christ. It means packing our bags, turning our backs on our former country and its government, and moving to the other side of the universe.

Paul has a favourite way of describing this massive change in our allegiance and in where we live. He calls it being 'in Christ'. It pops up in 2 Corinthians 5, just after the verses we've been discussing:

> Therefore, if anyone is *in Christ*, he is a new creation.
> The old has passed away; behold, the new has come.
> (2 Corinthians 5:17)

If we are 'in Christ'—if he is our Lord and representative—then we receive the benefits of what he has done *as if we ourselves had done it*. When he died on the cross, it was also our death; and when he rises from the dead, then we rise with him as well—to a life that is so new and different that Paul can call it "a new creation".

Can you begin to see why the love of Christ on the cross compels Paul to lead a totally different and radical life? *It's because his old life is over.* The rebellious sinful Paul who lived for himself and hated Christ—that Paul is now dead and buried with Christ. His sin has been judged, his death has taken place, and a new Paul has risen in place of the old Paul.

For sinners like us, this is news to celebrate. We all face the judgement and punishment that our sin deserves. We all face the death that comes to rebels against God. But if we are 'in Christ'—if he is the place we have moved to, the king to whom we now swear allegiance—then the death we deserve has already taken place. Jesus has died for all, and therefore all who are one with him have died as well. The old has passed away; the new has come. We now stand before God fresh and clean, like newborn babes, ready to begin a new life in his service.

This is the very purpose for which Christ died, Paul says: "and he died for all, that those who live might no longer live for themselves but for him who for their sake died and was raised" (v. 15).

If we are 'in Christ' then we live no longer for our own comfort, our own success, our own toys, our own fame, our own security, our own family, our own selves. We live *for him* who for our sake died and was raised. Whatever we do, whether in word or deed, we now do in the name of the Lord Jesus, our Master and Saviour (see Colossians 3:17).

To the rest of the world, this makes us look the teeniest bit nuts.

>>

When we leave the domain of darkness and move to the electorate of Jesus, we leave behind our old life, our old identity, our old plans and dreams. We begin a whole new existence, with a whole new reason for living.

There are multiple incentives. It's the best life. It's the life that fulfils the purpose that our creator has for us. It's the life, therefore, that brings real freedom, satisfaction and joy.

However, the most profound reason for pursuing the Christian life is that if we are in Christ, we have no other life to live. The old life is nailed to the cross of Jesus. It's dead and gone.

As we step into our new life in Christ, we are new people, with new identities, a new reason for living, and a new set of priorities in life. And as we step into this new life we are handed a fresh white sheet of paper with a fresh agenda written on it for our lives. It is God's agenda for us in this new life, and it contains just two words.

Jesus Christ.

Whatever we do in this new life—in our family, in our workplace, in our neighbourhood, in our church, in our society—we are to do it in honour of Jesus: to imitate him, to obey him, to rid ourselves of anything that dishonours him, to clothe ourselves in his character, to spread the knowledge and fame of him wherever we go.

Can you grasp this?

If you can, you have learnt what it means to be a Christian.

6

A question may now be nagging at you: If my old life is dead and gone, nailed to the cross with Christ, why does it still seem to be so alive and kicking?

Or to put it another way: I understand the logic of what Paul says in 2 Corinthians 5, but why don't I feel as compelled as he did?

This is certainly the reality of the Christian life. The habits and behaviours of our former life are still very much with us, like unwelcome old acquaintances who promise to stay only a night or two but are still there six weeks later, sleeping on the lounge and messing up the bathroom.

We do see changes in our lives as Christians, and we do not want to go back to how things were. And yet we seem to slip and fall so effortlessly. We find sin to be a stubbornly lingering presence, even though we know it does not belong in the new address we now occupy in Christ.

In fact, it's easy for those of us who have been Christians for some time—say, ten years or longer—to become quite used to the loitering reality of sin, to the point where we barely notice it any more. It is like a house renovation, undertaken with much initial enthusiasm and progress, that then gradually slows and declines, until the unfinished wall in the kids' bedroom and the half-installed second bathroom become the default state and no longer bother us. We don't even notice them after a while, and before we can muster the enthusiasm to even think (let alone do anything) about them again, other issues have arisen—the roof starts leaking, the laundry drain keeps getting blocked, and the paint on the door frames in the family room is all chipped thanks to collisions with toys.

The Christian life is like that. Even after many years of being 'in Christ', sin keeps reasserting itself at different points in our lives. We find anger and impatience welling up within us. Our love for others grows cold, and we retreat into our hobbies and pleasures. We succumb to greed and covetousness in wanting to keep up with the materialistic dreams of our neighbours and friends.

Why is it like this? More to the point, is there anything we can do about it? And how does the stubborn persistence of sin in our lives fit into the purpose that God has for us?

Happily, there is a quite extraordinary passage in the New Testament that answers these questions: the third chapter of Paul's letter to the Colossians.

≫

The premise of the long-running television show *Alias* was simple enough, and has been done many times in other ways. Sydney Bristow (Jennifer Garner) seemed like a normal young American 20-something, living a normal young American life with her family and friends. But in reality, Sydney was a super-competent field agent working for an ultra-secret intelligence organization, assuming multiple secret identities and generally glamorizing her way through a daring and dangerous operation every other week—all the while, of course, having to conceal her covert super-spy identity from her loved ones.

Sydney lived in two worlds, and the inevitable clashes and conflicts between them were a constant source of drama. Who, after all, was the real Sydney Bristow? Where did she really 'live'? Despite her occasional efforts to extract herself from the secret agent life and enjoy a normal safe everyday existence like everyone else, she was constantly drawn back to her 'other' identity. The subtext was not subtle. Sydney was never more truly herself than when she was adopting her various aliases and saving the world. This was who she really was, even though it was hidden from her family and friends.

With one or two important differences, this is pretty much how the apostle Paul describes the Christian life in Colossians 3.

To be a Christian is to be 'in Christ', in the sense that we explored in our previous chapter—that is, joined to him, one with him, living under his rule in his electorate, having him as our representative. And if we are 'in Christ', then we go where he goes. When he died, it was our death. And when he rose from the dead and ascended to the right hand of his Father in heaven… well, that's where we went too. Here's how Paul puts it:

> If then you have been raised with Christ, seek the things
> that are above, where Christ is, seated at the right hand

of God. Set your minds on things that are above, not on things that are on earth. For you have died, and your life is hidden with Christ in God. When Christ who is your life appears, then you also will appear with him in glory. (Colossians 3:1-4)

The implication is clear: Christians lead a double life. We've died to our old existence, and our true identity is now in Christ, seated at the right hand of God. *That's who we really are.* That's where our real life is—a secret life, hidden with Christ in God. And this truth about us, although currently concealed from the everyday world and the people we bump into each day, will one day be revealed for all to see when Christ returns in splendour.

In the meantime, we live with the same tension Sydney Bristow lived with. We still live in the everyday world. We still go to work and have family dinners and chat to our neighbours in the driveway. We are still involved in our old life, even though we know that our new heavenly life in Christ is where we belong. In particular, sin is still an everyday companion because we still live in a sin-soaked culture, and we still inhabit a body and a personality that is used to being selfish and rebelling against God.

Paul certainly isn't puzzled or surprised by the presence of sin in the Christian's life here on Earth. He regards it not as a conundrum but as an urgent challenge. That's why he urges the Colossians to "seek the things that are above" and to "set your minds on things that are above", and why he commands them in the rest of the chapter to exterminate the sin that remains in their lives:

> Put to death therefore what is earthly in you: sexual immorality, impurity, passion, evil desire, and covetousness, which is idolatry. On account of these the wrath of God is coming. In these you too once walked, when you were living in them. But now you must put them all away: anger, wrath, malice, slander, and obscene talk from your mouth. Do not lie to one another, seeing that you have put off the old self with its practices and have put on the new self, which is being renewed in knowledge after the image of its creator. (Colossians 3:5-10)

Your old life is gone, says Paul. You have shucked off your old self like a set of hideous and embarrassing old clothes, and have become a whole new self and identity in Christ. Your old life is dead; your new life is hidden with Christ in God. Therefore, live that way! Don't tolerate the words and deeds of your former life. Get rid of them. Kill them. They don't belong any more. By God's grace you have been rescued from the domain of darkness and transferred into the kingdom of the Son. So live in the light, not in the darkness.

This is where the logic of real Christianity is so different from the popular misconception. Christians strive to get rid of sin in their lives not in order to get to heaven, but because they already live there. We are driven to lead different lives here and now because our true life exists there and then.

Paul's language is strong because the challenge is urgent. The puritan John Owen was fond of saying, "You must be killing sin, or it will be killing you". These sinful behaviours are, after all, the very things that bring God's anger upon disobedient humanity. Are we willing, then, to tolerate them in our lives? To wink at them? To become familiar and comfortable with them?

The sad fact is that this urgent task tends to drift down our daily agenda. When was the last time you identified a sinful action or attitude in your life and took steps to kill it? Do you regard the old earthly habits and behaviours of your former life as an urgent problem to be addressed? Or has getting rid of sin in your life become like that renovation project you started all those years ago but that has now subsided into inactivity?

The sinful actions and attitudes that Paul lists cover all the common problems: impurity and immorality; lust and greed; anger and malice; lies and slander.

Perhaps for you the pressing problem is anger. Are you prone to flare up in hostility towards others when they get in your way? Are you easily riled, and likely to take out your frustrations on your family? If so, you need to get rid of this. Kill it off. You have no business living that way any more. It belongs to your old life, not your new life.

Or perhaps your big ongoing sin is greed. If so you would certainly not be alone, especially in our affluent Western churches. The love of luxury and possessions "is too much with us; late and soon/Getting and spending, we lay waste our powers" (as Wordsworth said). This is no way for someone to live whose real treasure is heavenly and eternal. It's ridiculous. Get rid of it. Kill it.

The question of *how* exactly we are to kill off the habits and vestiges of our old lives is another question, and we will return to it shortly.

But first we need to ponder the positive counterpart to killing sin in our lives.

>>

Paul not only wants the Colossians to get rid of the old clothes of their former life; he also wants them to put on a whole new outfit befitting their new lifestyle. He puts it like this:

> Put on then, as God's chosen ones, holy and beloved, compassionate hearts, kindness, humility, meekness, and patience, bearing with one another and, if one has a complaint against another, forgiving each other; as the Lord has forgiven you, so you also must forgive. And above all these put on love, which binds everything together in perfect harmony. And let the peace of Christ rule in your hearts, to which indeed you were called in one body. And be thankful. Let the word of Christ dwell in you richly, teaching and admonishing one another in all wisdom, singing psalms and hymns and spiritual songs, with thankfulness in your hearts to God. And whatever you do, in word or deed, do everything in the name of the Lord Jesus, giving thanks to God the Father through him. (Colossians 3:12-17)

Instead of anger, put on kindness; instead of frustration, patience; instead of whining, forbearance and thankfulness; instead of selfishness, compassion. And like a coat that goes over them all and finishes the whole outfit off perfectly: *love*.

'Love' is one of those broad and widely used words—like 'faith' and 'grace' and 'worship' and 'church'—where the first meaning that pops into our heads today is often not what the Bible is talking about when it uses the word.

We tend to think of love as a sentiment; something warm and soft and kind; or romantic and emotional. When we put the words 'truth' and 'love' together in a sentence, for example—as in 'tell the truth but do it in love'—we usually mean 'speak gently and kindly; don't be too strong or direct; take it easy'.

But this is not the essence of Christian 'love'. It may be loving to speak gently and kindly to someone, but in other circumstances love may require us to speak more forcefully and firmly. It would depend on what the other person really needed at that point—a gentle reminder or a stern talking to. There are times in life when we need each of these.

Love is not an emotional atmosphere or a sentiment. The death of Jesus shows us this. His death was not sweet, soft or romantic. It was an act of shocking brutality to which he walked with tears of blood. But it was the supreme and defining act of love. "By this we know love," says John, "that he laid down his life for us, and we ought to lay down our lives for the brothers" (1 John 3:16). John is echoing the words of Jesus himself at this point: "This is my commandment, that you love one another as I have loved you. Greater love has no-one than this, that someone lay down his life for his friends" (John 15:12-13).

Love is a determination to lay down our lives for our friends; to seek the benefit of others, even to our own cost. It is an orientation towards the other; a turning outward of our vision, away from what we want and crave and desire towards the person standing in front of us, and to what would help them grow and flourish.

Anger, impatience and complaining are all symptoms of an inwardly looking eye—one that sees only my interests, my frustration, my inconvenience, my failure, my inability to do and have what I want.

By contrast, kindness, patience and forbearance all spring from being more concerned about you and your wellbeing than me and my desires. They spring from what DB Knox was fond of calling 'other-person-centredness', and which the Bible simply calls 'love'.[4]

Love of course requires that I consider what might be for your wellbeing and benefit. Love is most effective when I perceive most clearly what would truly help you. This is why the love of the Father in giving his Son for us, and the love of the Son in laying down his life for us, is so monumental. It is the greatest love because it paid the greatest cost to meet our greatest need. John again: "In this the love of God was made manifest among us, that God sent his only Son into the world, so that we might live through him. In this is love, not that we have loved God but that he loved us and sent his Son to be the propitiation for our sins" (1 John 4:9-10).

Love is elemental to God's character. To love others is to be like God, and this is how God originally made us to be. He created us to be like him, in his image.

This is liberating to understand. In putting off sin and clothing ourselves instead in the character of Christ, we are not doing something strange or alien to our natures. We are in fact becoming more truly ourselves. As Paul puts it, we are "being renewed in knowledge after the image of [our] creator" (Colossians 3:10).

4 "God's goodness means that he is other-person-centred. He has created us in his image to be other-person-centred"—DB Knox, *The Everlasting God*, Matthias Media, Sydney, 2009, p. 50. For an extended discussion of how 'other-person-centredness' (or 'love') is the basis of all true relationship, beginning with God's relationship within the Trinity, see pages 165-172.

This is God's plan and purpose for us—to renew and restore his own likeness in us, as seen so perfectly in the character of his Son. It's to remake us as the humans we were meant to be, who live in love rather than selfishness, in integrity rather than deceit, in kindness and patience rather than anger and destructiveness. But this does not involve the removal of my personality and individuality. It's not the dissolving of who I am into a great ocean of divinity (as nirvana is for the Buddhist). Rather, God's purpose is the renovation and restoration and perfection of me in Christ. It's the creature finally becoming the marvellously unique person that the creator always intended.

This is God's grand cosmic purpose, and Colossians is not the only place it is mentioned. It is all over the New Testament:

> And we know that for those who love God all things work together for good, for those who are called according to his purpose. For those whom he foreknew he also predestined to be conformed to the image of his Son, in order that he might be the firstborn among many brothers. (Romans 8:28-29)

> For by grace you have been saved through faith. And this is not your own doing; it is the gift of God, not a result of works, so that no one may boast. For we are his workmanship, created in Christ Jesus for good works, which God prepared beforehand, that we should walk in them. (Ephesians 2:8-10)

> Now the Lord is the Spirit, and where the Spirit of the Lord is, there is freedom. And we all, with unveiled face, beholding the glory of the Lord, are being

transformed into the same image from one degree of glory to another. For this comes from the Lord who is the Spirit... For God, who said, "Let light shine out of darkness," has shone in our hearts to give the light of the knowledge of the glory of God in the face of Jesus Christ. (2 Corinthians 3:17-18, 4:6)

For the grace of God has appeared, bringing salvation for all people, training us to renounce ungodliness and worldly passions, and to live self-controlled, upright, and godly lives in the present age, waiting for our blessed hope, the appearing of the glory of our great God and Saviour Jesus Christ, who gave himself for us to redeem us from all lawlessness and to purify for himself a people for his own possession who are zealous for good works. (Titus 2:11-14)

God's purpose in uniting us with Christ in his death and raising us up to a new life with him is not that we would stay the same. It's that we would be *transformed* into the likeness of Christ, who is the image of God. It's that every word and deed of our everyday lives would be done in the name of Jesus. It's that our lives would be shot through with love, and with all the characteristics and actions that flow from that deep commitment to the good of others.

It's that we would become what we were always created to be: lovers of God and of our neighbour.

»

To put it another way, God's single purpose for our lives is Jesus: that we die with Jesus, that we rise with Jesus, that we are transferred into Jesus' kingdom, that we are transformed to be like Jesus.

For some of us, this may seem both too much and not enough.

At one level, it might feel like an impossibly grand and exalted purpose that I could never aspire to. My character is drastically short of the character of Jesus. And while putting off sin and putting on Christ's character sounds great in theory, how do I do that exactly? Where do I start? (More on this in our next chapter.)

However, somewhat perversely, some of you may be feeling a bit cheated at this point. This book opened with the promise of discussing the often-neglected big issues of life—of who I am, what my life is really about, what I am here for, and where I should head next. And you may be wondering: When are we going to get to the big stuff? When are we going to talk about work, for example, and what job or career I should pursue? When are we going to talk about marriage and family and relationships and finances and security, and all the rest? When are we going to deal with the nitty-gritty reality of tiredness and stress and dissatisfaction that I face every day? When are we going to get to the pressing issues that really concern me?

This is precisely where God's purposes collide with our own. I am vitally concerned with my work, my study, my family life, my money, my ambitions, my comfort, my security, and pretty much anything else that has the word 'my' in front of it. But what is God's purpose and priority for our lives?

It's not that we have a good and fulfilling career.

It's not that we build up financial security.

It's not that we find the perfect man or woman to marry.

It's not that we give our children the best in life.

It's not that we maintain a healthy body or lifestyle.

It's not that we enjoy all the good things of his creation.

And it's not even that we get involved at church and put ourselves on lots of rosters.

God's most important agenda item, under which everything else fits, is Jesus Christ. He wants to transfer us into *his* kingdom and transform us step by step to be like *him*, whose death was our death and whose life is now our life. He wants us to fix our eyes and hearts and minds not on all the earthly things that crowd our agenda, but on Christ above, where our true life is. And the consequence of this will be a consistent striving to put to death the sinfulness that belongs to this earthly life, and to clothe ourselves in the character of Jesus, the Lord of the age to come.

This all-important purpose will spill over into every part of our lives—our work, our family, our children, our money, our time, our relationships, our politics, our communities, and our church. In each of these areas, God wants us to be transformed into the image of our creator.

This is what truly matters to God. This is his purpose for our lives.

Can you believe this? Can you believe that it matters far more to God that you are transferred into the kingdom of Jesus than what particular job you have or where you live? Can you believe that it matters far more to God that your kids are transformed into the image of Jesus than that they get into the best schools or have fulfilling careers or get married?

If you can believe that then you can be a Christian, for that is what it really means to put our faith and trust in Christ. It means screwing up the piece of paper our own petty dreams and ambitions are written on, and gratefully accepting the one that God holds out to us—the one on which is written that single glorious word.

Jesus.

7

We've been looking at God's purpose for the world and for our lives: to transfer people into the kingdom of his Son, and transform people into his image. And we saw in our last chapter that this extraordinary and gracious work of God comes with an imperative—with an obligation, if you like. If by grace we have been transferred into Christ's kingdom, then we can no longer live as if our address is still in the domain of darkness. We must kill off the attitudes and practices of our former life, and replace them with a way of life that befits who we now really are 'in Christ'.

Those of a more practical nature are owed an explanation at this point. *How precisely are we meant to do this?* How do we kill off the old and put on the new? Given how stubbornly sin seems to hang around, and how far short of the character of Jesus we often are, this is a pressing question!

We're not the first ones, of course, to ponder it. Christians have always grappled with this question, and various solutions have been suggested over the centuries.

The monastic movement was one vast and drastic attempt to exclude sin from the Christian life, basically by excising Christians from the everyday world of sinners.

Behind the walls of the monastery, away from the pollution of the world, it was thought that devoted Christians might have some reasonable chance of staving off the temptations of the earthly nature.

In some streams of monasticism, the idea was not just to exclude society but also to subdue the body and dampen its desires. If the body itself could be brought under control —by denying it stimulation of the senses, by eating and sleeping in harsh conditions, by wearing uncomfortable clothing—then perhaps its desires and passions could also be reined in.

This impulse is as old as the New Testament itself. The scribes and Pharisees of Jesus' time thought that by scrupulously observing certain rituals and external practices, they could eliminate impurity from their lives. But Jesus pointed out the obvious—that impurity and evil are not just external to us but also lodged deep within us. We can't escape evil by, for example, preventing certain foods from entering our bodies. "For from within," says Jesus in Mark 7, "out of the heart of man, come evil thoughts, sexual immorality, theft, murder, adultery, coveting, wickedness, deceit, sensuality, envy, slander, pride, foolishness. All these evil things come from within, and they defile a person" (verses 21-23).

In Colossians, right at the end of chapter 2, Paul makes a similar sort of point about people who think that rules and regulations about what you can handle, taste or touch will be of any real benefit in restraining sin. Such practices look wise and impressive, Paul says, "in promoting self-made religion and asceticism and severity to the body, but they are of no value in stopping the indulgence of the flesh" (verse 23).

It's after this blast at the emptiness and uselessness of human religion that Paul turns in chapter 3 to how sinful behaviour is really changed. It's not by focusing on our bodies, as if by restraining them we can restrain sin. It's by focusing somewhere else entirely. Or rather, on someone else entirely.

If you have died with Christ and been raised with him, says Paul, then focus your attention *there*—on him. Set your minds on Christ, who is above, not on what is on earth. For your true self and your real life are hidden there in Christ.

This mental focus is the basis upon which Paul then says (in verse 5), "Put to death therefore what is earthly in you: sexual immorality, impurity…" and so on.

So the first step towards killing sin is not to restrain the body, but to redirect the mind.

»

What is your mind normally filled with?

I can usually tell when I've been working too hard, or am in need of a holiday. My mind starts to fill with daydreams of golf, and the fact that I haven't been playing any lately. I start to zone out in front of the computer, and mentally find myself standing on the picturesque sixth tee at St Michael's in Sydney's east, with a vista of the ocean and the course spread out before me, the sun not long up, a light breeze rippling my shirt sleeve, and a nice fat welcoming fairway to unleash a drive into (or at least in the vague direction of).

It's hardly strange that my writing output begins to decline as the mental golf increases (that last paragraph being a rare exception). Nor is it strange that the more my heart and mind are captivated by the goal I am seeking to reach—such as the book I'm trying to write—the more I get done.

Of course, our minds are not the only things that drive our actions. We humans are a complicated mess of inclinations, desires, emotions and needs. But deep at the core of our being lie the things we hold to be true, the mental pillars on which our worlds are constructed. We strongly believe these things and we build our lives upon them. They might be propositions like these:

- My wife loves me.
- If I'm going to be happy then I need to look out for my own best interests.
- More money will make my life better.
- Sydney is a better place to live than London.

These are things we *know*. They are not just facts we have heard or pieces of information stored away in our brains—these 'truths' are more basic than that. They reach down into the very foundations of our personality.

These basic beliefs form a very significant aspect of what the Bible refers to as the 'mind'—not just the thinking machine in our heads, but the things we deeply know and rely on to be true.

The problem is that as rebels against God, we embrace a whole number of 'earthly' or 'fleshly' ideas that are false and enslaving, that ruin our lives, and that eventually bring down the wrath of God on our heads. We lay down a big lie in the foundations of our thinking—that God is not really God, and that we can run our own lives without him—and it all goes wrong from that point on.

Killing off the earthly attitudes and actions that remain in our lives is in large measure a matter of changing our minds. As Paul puts it elsewhere, we are to be "transformed by the renewal of [our] mind" (Romans 12:2). God reconfigures our whole mind and character as we grasp and understand more deeply who we truly are in Christ, what he has done on our behalf, where our real life now resides, what is truly important in this life, and what the future holds.

Another way of saying all this is that the first and primary means by which God achieves his purpose in us is by speaking his truth into our misguided and deluded minds. As we've already seen in Colossians, it was through the powerful word of truth, the gospel, that the Colossians were transferred out of darkness and into the kingdom of the Son. Through his speech—his message, his truth, his word (as we often call it)—God reprograms and renews our minds.

Let us put this in practical terms. If we wish to make progress in renewing our lives in the image of our creator, we need to be active in the renewal of our minds. Do you make it a regular discipline to focus your thoughts and eyes and heart on where your life truly is, hidden in Christ above, waiting to be revealed? Or do the days go past without you pausing to direct your thoughts and attention to what is truly important, to the eternal kingdom you now belong to in Christ?

Regular Bible reading is, of course, the obvious way to do this. In fact, this is the real nature and value of reading and reflecting on the Bible as often as possible. We often think that our 20-minute early morning Scripture reading should always provide us with a little nugget of reassurance or promise, or with a simple point of application that we can put into practice today. And it often does. But the chief ongoing value of sustained regular Bible reading is simply that it constantly reorients and reprograms our minds with the truth. It renews our minds. It continually focuses our thoughts on Christ above, because Christ is the centrepiece and theme of the whole Bible. As we read and absorb what God is saying to us in the Bible, the old false ideas of our earthly lives are dismantled piece by piece, and a new, renovated mind is built instead.

Reading the Bible is not the only way to hear God's word and focus our minds above. We can listen to recorded sermons, read Christian books, pray over our notes from Sunday's preaching, follow Christian blogs, and more besides. There are many resources and options available.

But we have not mentioned the most enduring and valuable resource that God has provided to help us hear his word and focus our minds on Christ. This resource is not in audio, video, printed or electronic form. It is readily available but often not utilized. It is wonderfully effective but also sometimes frustrating.

It is each other.

>>

When Paul urged the Colossians to set their minds on Christ, he probably didn't picture them reading their Bibles every morning before breakfast, if for no other reason than that the New Testament didn't exist yet and the Old Testament wasn't available in personal editions for people to take to work on the train.

However, Paul did want the Colossians to hear the word of Christ deeply and often. He wanted that word to dwell in them "richly" (as he says in 3:16), and the means by which that was to happen was for them to *speak that word to each other* in mutual teaching, admonishment and song:

> Let the word of Christ dwell in you richly, teaching and admonishing one another in all wisdom, singing psalms and hymns and spiritual songs, with thankfulness in your hearts to God. (Colossians 3:16)

And so the other simple and immensely practical step we can take towards putting sin to death in our lives and clothing ourselves instead with the character of Christ, is to *keep speaking the truth of Christ to each other, whenever and however we can.*

This doesn't have to be formalized, but it can be. It can be the nightly chat around the dinner table, the one-to-one meeting with a friend to read the Bible and pray, the small group that meets regularly for Bible encouragement, or the larger Sunday gathering where the whole congregation meets. Any time and any place is a good opportunity to speak a word of encouragement, exhortation or even admonishment to our brothers and sisters.

The writer to the Hebrews urged his readers to do this mutual ministry daily, because the pressing danger of sin is so serious:

> Take care, brothers, lest there be in any of you an evil, unbelieving heart, leading you to fall away from the living God. But exhort one another every day, as long as it is called 'today', that none of you may be hardened by the deceitfulness of sin. (Hebrews 3:12-13)

We will return to this subject more fully in our next chapter, but here is the most basic and obvious way for all Christians to be part of God's purposes in the world—by teaching, urging, exhorting, encouraging and admonishing one another to abandon the false and stupid ideas of our earthly brains and fill our minds instead with thoughts of Christ above.

God has given us each other as living, breathing channels for the word of Christ to be spoken. If we desire to get rid of sin in our lives and clothe ourselves in the character of Christ, then we have both an opportunity and a responsibility. We should grasp whatever chance we get to be taught, encouraged and helped by our brothers and sisters; and we should take seriously our role and responsibility to do the same for others.

Do you see this as an everyday personal responsibility and ministry?

»

So God is achieving his Christ-centred plans in the world using two great methods or means: by redirecting and renewing our minds through his powerful word; and by the fellowship of Christ's people, who speak that word to each other in teaching, admonishing, encouraging and exhorting.

However, there is a third vital means that we haven't yet mentioned.

We see it in Colossians 1 where Paul *thanks God* for the way the gospel has born fruit in the Colossians' lives (in verse 3), and then *prays* earnestly and constantly that this fruit would grow and blossom in their lives—in the form of greater understanding, wisdom, worthy living, patience, thanksgiving and joy (in verses 9-12). Paul credits God himself with their response, and prays for God to work in them to nourish and grow that response into a transformed life.

Paul knew that he could speak the word of God to people until they (and he) were blue in the face. But because of the perversity and stubbornness of the human heart, those words would be without effect unless something changed within—unless Someone softened their hard hearts, opened their blind eyes, and moved their stubborn wills to respond.

This is the third means by which God changes our lives—through the internal operation of his own Spirit in response to our prayers. If we wish to put sin to death in our lives, we need to pray for God to keep changing us from the inside out, by his Spirit. If we wish to see our friends and neighbours come to Christ and become united with him, we need to beg God to work in their hearts, by his Spirit. If we wish to see our Christian brothers and sisters persevere in Christ, and grow in their knowledge of him, and put off the sin that still clings to them—we need to pray that God would keep working within them, by his Spirit.

There is a Latin phrase that describes the essential place of God's own work by his Spirit in bringing change to people's lives: *sine qua non*. It means, literally, 'without which not'. So meat is a *sine qua non* for meat pies. Patience is a *sine qua non* for raising children or playing golf. And the internal work of God's Spirit is a *sine qua non* for the progress of God's agenda in the world. No-one becomes a Christian, or grows to maturity as a Christian, without God being at work in their hearts.

We all know that this is true. At an intellectual level we understand the absolute necessity of calling upon God to back up our speaking of his word with the illuminating and life-giving work of his Spirit. We can also acknowledge what an unspeakable privilege it is to be able to call the God of the universe into action (as it were)—to have him answer our prayers and change the hearts and minds of those we are praying for.

And yet we are so slow and unwilling to pray. We forget, we get distracted, we get too busy, we get lazy. We become so absorbed in all that *we* are doing to move ourselves and others forward in Christ that we neglect the crucial importance of God's Spirit being at work, and so we also neglect to pray.

In fact, perhaps that is the very best thing we can do at this moment: pray.

Father,

It is stupid and small-minded of us not to pray. It shows up how little we trust your promise and power to change people's hearts by your Spirit. It reveals our self-centredness and laziness, and our unwillingness to give our time to an activity that is neither visible to others nor tangible in its immediate results.

Forgive us, Lord, for our neglect. Forgive us our disobedience, for you urge and command us to pray, and yet we often fail to.

Give to us, we beg, the spirit of Daniel, who prayed so faithfully when under so much pressure not to; give us

*the spirit of Elijah, who depended on you so earnestly
when all seemed lost; give us the spirit of Paul, who
drenched all his many gospel labours in a prayerful
dependence on your Spirit; give us the spirit of Jesus,
who taught us to pray and showed us the greatest
example of prayerful trust in his Father.*

Amen

>>

There is nothing particularly revolutionary or flashy or radical about the three means by which God is working to achieve his agenda in the world. He uses his word spoken by his people in prayerful dependence on his Spirit.

This simple recipe for change and growth is easy to understand, but hard to follow consistently. So many alternatives present themselves as better or faster paths to growth; so many distractions divert us from this straightforward road; so many weaknesses in our own souls cause us to turn aside or give up when the going gets tough.

But if we are to make progress in advancing God's agenda in our own lives, not to mention in the lives of others around us, then these three simple weapons are God's extraordinary gift to us: his word, his Spirit, his people.

8

In our last chapter, we looked at the three basic means or methods by which God is achieving his purpose in our world and in our lives:

- He renews and redirects our minds through his true and powerful word.
- He opens our blind eyes and resurrects our dead hearts through his life-giving Spirit.
- And, remarkably, he uses ordinary people like us—people who speak his word to others, and people who pray for his Spirit to work in other people's hearts.

We need to explore that third point a little more, because for many of us this is a challenge to our self-perception. We don't think of ourselves as channels for God's powerful word. We tend to leave that sort of thing to the professionals: to the pastors and elders and theologians and evangelists. They're the ones with the training, after all. We're happy to pray for people, although we don't get around to it all that often. And we're even happy to invite our friends along to things so that they can hear the professionals speak.

But everyday Christians like us as *speakers* of God's word? That feels like a decidedly more uncomfortable and distant possibility. We feel weak and inadequate for the task. We aren't any good at making clever or fine-sounding arguments. And we often lack boldness in speaking out in the midst of a hostile or apathetic community.

But strangely and wonderfully, that is how nearly all speakers of God's word feel most of the time. It's certainly how Paul portrays himself in his letters to the Christians in Corinth. In contrast to some of the orators he was being compared with, Paul was happy to admit that he was an unimpressive speaker who delivered his message "in weakness and in fear and much trembling" (1 Corinthians 2:3; see also 2 Corinthians 10:10). His audience reacted to his message with derision, despising it as either stupid or weak (1 Corinthians 1:18-25). But in the depths of his weakness and inadequacy, God's grace was sufficient for Paul (2 Corinthians 12:9). In fact, the fragile, weak, fading, mortal nature of the container made the treasure it contained all the more glorious: "We have this treasure in jars of clay," says Paul, "to show that the surpassing power belongs to God and not to us" (2 Corinthians 4:7).

Being weak and inadequate is not an excuse for avoiding God's purpose; it is virtually a requirement for being part of it.

But, you might say, that was Paul. He was a hero of the faith. I am anything but! Surely God uses gifted people like pastors and evangelists to speak his word. Is it really necessary to include *me* in that part of the task?

There's no question that 'ministry leaders' (if I can call them that) play a vital and important role in the spread of the gospel and the growth of disciples—they do now as they did in the early church. In Colossians (where we've been spending a bit of time), we see that the gospel first came to Colossae via Epaphras, who is one of Paul's colleagues. It's also clear that Paul himself had an important public ministry, not only via his letters and encouragement to the churches but also in his constant proclamation of the gospel message in the face of severe opposition. And he asks the Colossians to pray for that ministry (in Colossians 4:3-4).

However, the word ministry of Paul and Epaphras does not exhaust the possibilities. Just because they had a leading and important role to play, doesn't mean they did all the work. Colossians itself makes this clear. In that beautiful passage in chapter 3 about putting off sin and putting on the clothes of Christ, Paul urges the Colossians to "let the word of Christ dwell in you richly, teaching and admonishing one another in all wisdom, singing psalms and hymns and spiritual songs, with thankfulness in your hearts to God" (Colossians 3:16).

The rich presence of Christ's word in their midst was expressed in mutual teaching and admonishing with all wisdom, and in glad, thankful singing. It also resulted in them speaking differently with outsiders. They were not only to pray for Paul's ministry of proclamation but to dabble regularly in it themselves: "Walk in wisdom toward outsiders, making the best use of the time. Let your speech always be gracious, seasoned with salt, so that you may know how you ought to answer each person" (Colossians 4:5-6).

The expectation seems to be that if we are transferred into Christ's kingdom, and if we set our minds on Christ and are steadily transformed into Christ's image, then we will also have Christ's word on our lips.

Which makes sense when you think about it.

»

Spirit-filled people speak differently. This is one of the characteristics of those who are in Christ, who have died with him and been raised with him to a new life. We are liberated not only to live a new life but also to speak new words.

This is because our words are an outpouring of who we are. As Jesus says, "The good person out of the good treasure of his heart produces good, and the evil person out of his evil treasure produces evil, for out of the abundance of the heart his mouth speaks" (Luke 6:45). We speak new words because we have a new heart that is filled with the Spirit of Christ.

This is what we should expect; because the characteristic activity of a Spirit-filled person, throughout the Bible, is that they speak forth the words of God—that they 'prophesy'. When God takes some of the Spirit that was on Moses, and puts it on the 70 elders, they break into prophecy, although it doesn't last (Numbers 11:25). And when Joshua wants Moses to stop Eldad and Medad prophesying, Moses replies (I think with a hint of exasperation in his voice), "Are you jealous for my sake? Would that all the LORD's people were prophets, that the LORD would put his Spirit on them!" (Numbers 11:29).

Moses' wish comes true at Pentecost in Acts 2. As the Spirit falls upon all the gathered disciples, they begin to tell forth "the mighty works of God" in the languages of the nations that are gathered in Jerusalem (Acts 2:11). And when Peter explains to the stunned crowd what is going on, he makes clear that this extraordinary event is the fulfilment of the Old Testament hope that one day God would indeed put his Spirit on all his people, and that they would all prophesy: "And in the last days it shall be, God declares, that I will pour out my Spirit on all flesh, and your sons and your daughters shall prophesy…" (Acts 2:17, quoting Joel 2:28).

A few chapters later in Acts, the disciples are again gathered, and again the Spirit falls upon them, and again the result is speaking the word of God (i.e. prophecy): "And when they had prayed, the place in which they were gathered together was shaken, and they were all filled with the Holy Spirit and continued to speak the word of God with boldness" (Acts 4:31).

What they had begun to do at Pentecost they continued to do through the work of the Spirit.

This Spirit-impelled speech also continues to feature in the early church, as the New Testament epistles describe it. In particular, the important passage in 1 Corinthians 12-14 describes and regulates this Spirit-filled speech. In 12:1-3, the Spirit opens our mouths to declare that Jesus is Lord—because only the Spirit can change our hearts to willingly submit to Jesus as Lord, and our mouths only reflect what is in our hearts. As the chapters unfold, Paul explains that because we have all been baptized by and in the one Spirit, we should manifest or give expression to the Spirit's presence by acting in love for the common good. In particular, he urges us to be zealous for prophecy, because by prophecy (that is, speaking the word of the Lord under the power of the Spirit) we encourage and build others, including the outsider in our midst (14:24-25). Paul expects the Corinthians to come to their gatherings with intelligible words to say (whether in the form of "a hymn, a lesson, a revelation, a tongue, or an interpretation"), and he wants them to use these words for edification or 'building' (14:26).

The same picture emerges elsewhere in the New Testament:

- In Ephesians 4, the result of the Christ's work in us through the Spirit is that we speak the truth in love to one another and to our neighbours (verses 15, 25); our speech should be adapted to the need of the occasion, and have one aim in mind: "that it may give grace to those who hear" (verse 29).
- One chapter later in Ephesians, Paul urges us to be filled by the Spirit, with the result that we speak to one another (in psalms, hymns and spiritual songs) and give thanks to God always and for everything (5:18-20).
- In Romans 15:14-15, Paul affirms that the Christians he is writing to are "full of goodness, filled with all knowledge and able to instruct one another". His letter is not a replacement for their mutual instruction, but "on some points I have written to you very boldly by way of reminder, because of the grace given me by God".
- In Philippians, Paul is very grateful to God for the partnership of the Philippians in all the different aspects of his ministry—in prayer, in suffering, in finances, but also in "the defence and confirmation of the gospel" (1:7). He is delighted that his imprisonment has actually

emboldened his fellow Christians to keep speaking God's word: "most of the brothers, having become confident in the Lord by my imprisonment, are much more bold to speak the word without fear" (1:14).

- In Hebrews 3, in the middle of a long section about the power and importance of God's word, the author urges his readers to "exhort one another every day, as long as it is called 'today', that none of you may be hardened by the deceitfulness of sin" (3:13). Later he says that this mutual exhortation and encouragement is one of the basic reasons for gathering together in church: "And let us consider how to stir up one another to love and good works, not neglecting to meet together, as is the habit of some, but encouraging one another, and all the more as you see the Day drawing near" (10:24-25).

This is the consistent testimony of the New Testament— that God uses not just 'professionals' to speak his word (like pastors and prophets and evangelists), but all of his people.

To put it another way, when we die with Christ and are raised with him, God radically reshapes us at the deepest level by his Spirit; at the level of what the Bible calls our 'heart'—the centre of our thoughts and will and personality. He springs us from the dark and delusional prison we were trapped in. He fills our hearts with his own presence, with his Spirit, and sets us free to live under the bright blue sky of the truth. And so the words that flow from our mouths are the words of free men and women, who know at last the truth about themselves and God and the world and the future; the truth about love and family and relationships; the truth about work and play and culture.

Christ-centred, Christ-exalting, Christ-filled speech is simply an exercise of the freedom of the Christian. It will be varied —as varied as we are in our abilities, our education, our background, our circumstances, our opportunities—but it will also be a universal consequence of being filled by the Spirit.

It will be a basic everyday consequence of being a disciple of Jesus.

>>

Disciples of Jesus come in a shocking array of shapes and sizes, not to mention ages, colours, personalities, cultures, families, abilities, opportunities and levels of maturity.

But it's also true to say that disciples of Jesus only come in one variety: the kind who say no to themselves, and take up their cross and lose their life with Jesus at Calvary; the kind who are raised to a new life in service of the Christ who died for them; the kind who have been charged and commissioned by the risen Lord Jesus to make disciples of all nations.

The 'Great Commission' in Matthew 28 could also be called simply the 'Disciples' Commission'. It was not given to a special or higher class of disciple, but to the small band of half-doubting, half-joyful followers who met Jesus on the mountain as he had directed them. And to this ragtag and by no means impressive group, Jesus issued a set of marching orders that has rung out around the world and down the centuries:

> "All authority in heaven and on earth has been given
> to me. Go therefore and make disciples of all nations,
> baptizing them in the name of the Father and of the
> Son and of the Holy Spirit, teaching them to observe all
> that I have commanded you. And behold, I am with you
> always, to the end of the age." (Matthew 28:18-20)

This isn't the time to chew over all that is rich and nourishing in this famous passage, but I'd like to think about three points that are important for our discussion.

The first is that the radical call to serve Jesus as disciple-makers stems from his universal authority. He is our Lord whose every command we long to obey, but he is also the supreme authority in all the world. Everyone should turn to him, stop rebelling against him, submit to him, long to serve him, give all their allegiance to him—everyone, in other words, should be his disciple.

In a world with multiple religions and multiple people groups, this is a radical statement—and it was as radical in the first century as it is in ours. Next time you're chatting in the lunchroom at work, try expressing the view that there is only one true God, and that he has crowned his Son Jesus with all authority, and that all peoples from all nations should become Jesus' disciples. Incredulity, hostility or awkward embarrassed silence are the most likely responses. You just can't say things like this in polite company. No-one has the right to say that one religion is better than another, let alone to suggest that only one of them is true. This is another of the very few beliefs that modern Western people share: the conviction that everyone should be left alone to believe 'whatever is true for them'. Diversity in belief and conviction is seen as a social virtue to be cultivated.

Christians can't help but be affected by this. No-one enjoys being labelled a bigot or a fanatic. And we often respond by keeping our heads down, sticking to our churches and fellowships, and making the occasional half-baked and semi-embarrassed effort at outreach. Or, if we do get more actively involved in the community and try to be connected and a blessing to those around us, we never get around to the part where we call on all nations to repent and put their faith in the one and only Lord of the world—because that tends to lead to some people getting offended or upset. We build lots of bridges but never cross them. And for that, the world will tolerate us and even thank us for making a positive contribution. But they will stay on their side of the bridge, and eventually bow before the authority of Jesus not as a disciple but as a rebel.

Secondly, we should notice that Jesus' command is not only universal in its scope; it is also universal in its application. It is a command not just for the first eleven disciples but also for every disciple—if only because the time scale involved requires it. Jesus promises that he will be with his disciples always as they make disciples, even "to the end of the age". The work of disciple-making is the central and abiding task of Jesus' disciples from the time of his resurrection and ascension until the time he returns at the end of the age. It has been going on, so far, for 2000 years—which would be rather difficult if the job was only for the eleven disciples who were there to hear the command when it was originally given.

The very nature of the disciple-making task means

that it generates not only new disciples, but new disciple-makers. New disciples were to be taught to obey everything that the Lord Jesus Christ commanded. And it is hard to imagine a more significant or important command of Jesus than this one—his parting charge to his disciples to make disciples of all nations. New disciples fall under exactly the same obligation as the original eleven disciples—they are to obey Jesus' command to get on with the job of making disciples, by announcing the gospel of his lordship to all nations and seeing people grow to maturity as servants of the Lord Jesus Christ.

Thirdly, the structure of the commission shows us that the task has two dimensions: initiating the nations into the triune God (that is, baptizing them—the mode or exact nature of which we can leave for another time!), and teaching them to obey Jesus' teachings. This corresponds to the two dimensions of God's purpose that we saw earlier: to transfer forgiven sinners into the kingdom of the Son, and then to transform them into the image of the Son as they put off sin and clothe themselves in his character.

In other words, 'making disciples' is not a one-off or instantaneous event. It doesn't just involve conversion or initiation into Christ; it also involves growth and maturity as a disciple, as new disciples learn to obey everything that Jesus has commanded. We often associate disciple-making with evangelism and conversion, but it is much more comprehensive than that. It involves everything from our initial conversations with a non-Christian friend right through to our encouragement of someone who has been a Christian for 50 years.

This is worth teasing out, because if we think of 'disciple-making' as a continuous process rather than a one-off event, it helps us to see how all of us—regardless of our talents or opportunities—can be involved in God's disciple-making program.

We could think of this process in a simple way using the following diagram:

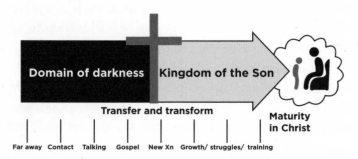

This diagram expresses the truth that, at one level, there are only two kinds of people in the world: those still stuck in the domain of darkness, and those who have been transferred into the kingdom of the Son through the work of the cross.

However, within those two broad categories there are common stages or phases that most people go through as they become a disciple and grow as a disciple.

Starting at the far left, some are *far away*, with no knowledge of the gospel, and no contact with Christian people or Christian teaching. They may be utterly ignorant or apathetic towards God, or even actively hostile towards him.

Some have made *contact* with a Christian person, or know something vaguely about Christ. They may have bumped into Christians through work or family or friendship. They may have had some loose connection with Christianity, via school or church when they were young.

Others have started *talking*, perhaps about spiritual or moral issues. They have begun to think, to ask questions and to have genuine conversations with the Christians they're in contact with.

And then we get to the point where people actually hear the *gospel* clearly explained—and with God's work in their heart they turn to Christ for the forgiveness of their sins, and are transferred from darkness to light and into the kingdom of the Son.

They are now *new Christians*, needing plenty of support and encouragement and teaching to establish them secure and strong in the faith.

Then comes the *growth* and maturing that continues throughout our Christian lives—a process that involves frequent *struggles* and setbacks as we battle against sin in our lives and against the constant effects of sin in our world.

And as part of that lifelong growth—and it may be quite early in the process, depending on our circumstances—we grasp the idea that being a disciple is also about being a disciple-maker; that our joyful privilege is not only to grow towards maturity, but also to go back to the left and give a helping hand to others, to seek to move them forward towards Christ and towards maturity in him. To be involved in this, most people will need some *training* to equip them with knowledge and skills and confidence to move others forward towards Christ.

Being a disciple, to use the shape of this diagram, means constantly seeking to move to the right, towards maturity in Christ. This happens, remember, through God's word and prayer—through setting our minds on Christ, and praying for his Spirit to work in us as we put sin to death and clothe ourselves with Christ's character. But as we move to the right, we realize that Christian love drives us also to go back to the left—to make contact with those who are far away, and talk to them and share the gospel with them, and follow them up as new Christians, and encourage them for their growth.

This is what a 'disciple-maker' is—someone who through the love of Christ is committed not only to 'moving to the right' themselves but also to helping everyone around them take one step to the right, no matter where they are on the spectrum.

Now this doesn't mean that we are all preachers with a capital P, or that we are all gifted evangelists who can speak to crowds. We will all have our own strengths and abilities and opportunities, and so we will each find our own way of moving others to the right by sharing God's word with them. There is a multitude of different possibilities, because there is a multitude of us, not to mention a multitude of people all around us needing to take a step to the right.

Let me give just a few examples of what I mean.

You're talking after church with someone, and rather than just chatting about how the week has been or what the kids are up to, you say something like, "You know, I really like the point the pastor made today when he said that our greatest need is for forgiveness. What did you think of that?" And you proceed to talk together about the word that was preached. You might even conclude by saying a short word of prayer or thanksgiving together.

Now, the question you have asked is just a short and simple question, but it opens up a conversation that dwells on the word, and encourages another person. It encourages them not only because you dwell on the word together, but also because they see your interest and willingness to set your mind on Christ. This ministry of personal conversation and encouragement is one that the pastor cannot have—not with a 120 different people on a Sunday morning. This is an act of disciple-making that only you can have, because you are the one standing opposite a person that God wants to see move to the right.

Let's take a weekday example. Your workmate is not a Christian, but he knows that you are. So far, you haven't had many conversations touching on spiritual issues. On this particular Monday, he asks you what you did on the weekend, and rather than mentioning everything else you did except church, you say that you heard a really stimulating sermon in church about how the world's greatest need is for forgiveness. And your workmate says, "Really? What about child poverty?" And you end up having a conversation about why our physical needs and problems are not the only ones we have, what forgiveness really is… and who knows what else. The conversation might range far and wide. You may get somewhere or you may not. But you've started talking with your friend. He has started to move from simply having *contact* with a Christian to *talking* about Christian issues.

Remember, God will do the work in people's hearts, not us. Our job is to seek in love to move people forwards by speaking the word in whatever way we can, in whatever context we can, to any person we can (whether they're a

Christian or not), praying that God would use our word (no matter how small it might be) to help that person make progress towards Christ, and towards maturity in Christ.

These first two examples have been instances of personal, spontaneous, everyday conversation in which we speak a word in order to encourage another person and (God willing) see them take a step forward. But the task of making disciples need not only be spontaneous and individual; it can also be more structured and planned; and we can also get together with others to work as a team. So for example:

- You might decide to meet one-to-one with a younger Christian at church to read the Bible and pray together each week for three months.
- Together with your spouse, you might decide to work out a regular Bible-reading pattern for the next six months as part of your family life.
- The small home group you are part of at church is a regular opportunity to meet with others to speak God's word to one another and pray. And so you go along each week, prepared and ready to speak for the benefit of others.
- Your small home group might also decide to work together to reach out to others, and move them to the right; you might decide to run an evangelistic program or course together to which you can invite your non-Christian friends.

The possibilities are limited only by our imaginations, and by our willingness to commit ourselves to the commission that our Lord has given us: to love people enough to help them move to the right.

9

The thing is: our lives do have a purpose and a meaning. There is a foundational and central truth that defines who we are and what our lives are really about.

Over the past several chapters, we've been trying to name what this 'thing' is.

We have seen that as a consequence of us being creatures made by a sovereign creator God, our meaning and purpose in life can only come from outside—from the God who designed and made us. We have also discovered that this purpose of God for us and for our world answers the seemingly impossible problems that we've made for ourselves through our rebellion against him. And we've seen that it is all centred on his Son, Jesus, and the new and everlasting kingdom that he is bringing. Through dying with Jesus and rising to a new life, we become members of that kingdom and are steadily transformed to be like him in holiness and godliness and love.

If we were to summarize these massive ideas into a simple statement that expressed God's purpose for the world and for our lives, it might go something like this:

Because God's grand purpose for his creation is
- *to transfer forgiven rebels into his Son's kingdom*
- *and to transform them into his Son's image*

then his purpose for my life is that I should
- *die with Christ and rise to new life in his kingdom*
- *press forward to maturity in Christ by putting sin to death and putting on the character of Christ*
- *in love, help others move from wherever they are towards maturity in Christ by prayerfully speaking God's word to them.*

Those last three statements are really a summary of what it means to be a Christian. It means living a new life in Christ that reaches into every corner of our daily existence.

But that is not how many Christians think about it. For many of us, 'Christianity' is one of many balls we are juggling. We are busy with life—with study or friends or kids or work or sport or music or family or relationships or politics or whatever it is that that gets us up in the mornings and fills our days. In the midst of this whirl, God-and-Jesus-and-church is just one of the responsibilities or interests competing for our precious time and resources. It's one of the balls we are juggling. We try to fit in as much 'church stuff' as we can, and feel a bit guilty that it's not always a higher priority. And we think that becoming a 'better' Christian would mean juggling the balls a bit differently so as to give a higher place on our agenda to certain activities—such as Bible reading or prayer or going to church or being involved in church activities.

But the thing is: God is not a ball (as a friend of mine once said to me in a moment of insight). We can't treat

God as if he is one of the balls we are juggling in life. The situation is entirely the reverse.

If all we've seen so far is true, God's purpose for our lives doesn't compete for attention alongside all the other things we have on our own personal agenda. *God's agenda completely rewrites and replaces ours.* His agenda sits over everything we do in life, and determines how we think about each aspect of our lives.

God is not a ball in our hands to be juggled. He is the Creator, the Master, the Sovereign Ruler of everything. We are the balls of clay crafted by his hands. It is not a question of juggling him into our busy lives. Rather, his purpose shows us how to live in his creation.

>>

Take *family* as an example.

Family life is one of God's good gifts. It is a wonderful part of the creation that God has put us in, although like all aspects of God's creation it is marred by sin.

Now, in nurturing and caring for our families, it's not that we have to divide our time between family and God—as if God and our families are competitors; as if we enter into some sort of negotiation with God as to how much time we're going to devote to his purpose for our lives and how much to family.

God's purpose overlays and permeates every aspect of our lives. It shows us *how* to care for our families, what's truly important for the members of our families, and what our priorities should be in family life.

In my role as a father, for example, God wants me to press forward towards maturity in Christ. He wants me to be patient with my children, to love them, to be slow to anger, to avoid exasperating them, to discipline them, to teach them, and so much more. He wants me to be a father of Christlike character.

God's plans also decisively shape my plans for my family. I want my wife and children to come to Christ as well, and to grow to maturity in him. I want to help them 'move to the right', just as I am seeking to move to the right in my own walk with Christ. This means reading the Bible with my family, praying for and with them, talking with them in the everyday hassles of life about what it means to live for Christ, and seeking to model this for them.

Pretty much everything else in family life is a minor detail that doesn't make much difference to this overriding purpose of God. Where we live, where we go on holidays, what toys we buy them—all these things are flexible and relatively unimportant compared with God's agenda for our families.

However, what do we typically do? We elevate the less important things to the very top of our list. It matters to us very much that we live in a really nice house in a nice suburb, and that we send our kids to the best schools. And so we work long hours—often both parents work long hours—in order to pay for these supposedly vital commodities. And we send our kids to tutoring colleges on the weekend so they can achieve better results, and we enrol them in lots of sporting and other activities so they can have every opportunity to succeed.

The result of course is that we are all constantly tired, hassled and pressured, and we have no time or energy to fulfil *God's* purpose in our families. What's more, we model to our kids that the truly important things in life—the things worth sacrificing for—are material possessions, a big house, and the best education.

In other words, we do what humanity has always done. We take God's good creational gifts, assert our own purposes over them, and rebel against the purpose and agenda God has for us.

We could say the same thing about work, about sport and leisure, about education, about food, about sex and marriage—about any of the good things God has given us in his creation. In each case, God's purpose is not something separate that we bolt onto our lives; it *governs* the way we live every part of our lives, every day.

In fact, we could even construct a simple template that expresses how this applies to the different areas of our daily lives. Let's try it with work:

A. Work is a good creation of God for our benefit and growth. And even though **work** is marred by sin and the Fall, we still find joy and satisfaction in it, and should receive it as God's good gift with thanksgiving.

B. It is possible to misuse this gift by using our devotion to **work** to assert our independence from God; by making success and satisfaction in our **work** the real goal and agenda of our lives; by partitioning our **work** off from God and his agenda for our lives.

C. But God's plan is for every aspect of our lives. It overlays and permeates everything we do. So God wants us to view our **work** as one of the areas in life in which we pursue his agenda, not ours—by pursuing Christlikeness in all that we do at **work**, and by seeking to move others in our **workplace** towards Christ as we relate to them.

D. This influences not only how we behave in our **workplace**, but also the decisions we make about **work**— how much time we devote to it, how ambitiously we pursue it, and what we're prepared to give up in order to gain success.

Now try reading back over those four points and replacing '**work**' with '**family**'. Now try it with '**love and marriage**'; and with your favourite leisure pastime. Try it with '**education**'. Try it with '**money**'.

Every aspect of our lives in this creation is subject to the same tension—the desire we have to assert our own purposes and agenda (the attitude otherwise known as 'sin') in defiance of God's purposes for us in Christ. And every aspect of our lives would be better, more satisfying, and more a source of joy-amidst-struggle if we were to submit to God's purposes rather than foolishly insist on our own.

>>

I have written a number of books about the Christian faith over the past 25 years, and read many more. I have noticed that these sorts of books often finish in a particular way—with an inspiring quote perhaps, or a heart-warming story, or a personal anecdote that captures the main idea. The author wants to end with a flourish, with something upbeat or memorable that readers can take with them once the book is closed and put back on the shelf, and the conversation between author and reader comes to an end.

My problem is that I don't want the conversation to end, because I know what you're like. I know what you're like because I am precisely the same.

I read books like this one, and (at least occasionally) get excited and enthused about what I've just read. I see the truth of what has been written, and I want to embrace it. I want to change my mind, and my life.

And yet this feeling fades. Life presses in. I start to forget what I've read, and my mind and life inexorably default back to what they were.

Ironically, this is precisely what we should expect as Christians, if what we've seen in the preceding chapters is true (especially chapter 6). The old life remains stubbornly with us. Sin is an ongoing presence, and if we are going to change it, we need to take ongoing action. We need to keep putting our old attitudes and behaviours and thought-patterns to the sword, and clothing ourselves instead with a new way of thinking and acting and being. And (as we saw) one of the key weapons God has given us for this task is *each other*.

So I'd like to close not with a story or a quote but with a plea to keep the conversation going—not with me, because this book is very soon to end, but with your brothers and sisters. God has given us each other—to speak his word to each other, to confess our sins to each other, to teach and encourage and admonish and support each other. If the insights and truths we have seen together from the Bible are to take root and bring change in our lives, we need the constant stimulus and encouragement of one another to keep going and growing.

Practically this could mean any number of things. Let me suggest just three ideas to get you thinking.

- At the simplest level, you could get together with a friend to re-read this book, discuss the contents together chapter by chapter, pray for one another, and help one another put the ideas into practice.
- You could meet with a friend for a weekly one-to-one meeting, and read together all the Bible passages that have been quoted or referenced in this book (they are listed in appendix 1). You could delve into them for yourselves, and pray about their implications for your lives.
- I have written a program called *The Course of Your Life*, which deals with many of the ideas in this book in a way that a small group can work through and discuss over a few months.[5] You could try using this program in a small group at church, or in your family. (For a list of other useful resources that are closely related to the ideas in this book, and which give them practical expression, see appendix 2.)

It doesn't really matter how you keep going and growing. What does matter is that we all encourage, exhort and spur one another on to 'move to the right'—to be transferred into Christ's kingdom and to be transformed to be like him.

Because that's the thing.

---

5   Available from matthiasmedia.com.

Appendix 1

One vital way to let God's extraordinary purposes for our lives penetrate further into our minds and hearts is simply to read and meditate upon his word. Below is a collection of all the Bible passages referenced in this book (listed by the chapter in which they appear and mostly in the order in which they appear). Try reading through these, perhaps with a friend, and pray that God would use his word to transform and renew your mind.

Chapter 2
Genesis 1-2
Isaiah 45:1-13

Chapter 3
Genesis 3
Ecclesiastes 3
James 4:13-16

Chapter 4
Colossians 1
Ephesians 2:4-5
Philippians 2:9-11

Chapter 5
2 Corinthians 11:21-29, 5:14-17
1 Peter 2:20-24
Isaiah 53:5
Colossians 3:17

Chapter 6

Colossians 3:1-17
1 John 3:16
John 15:12-13
1 John 4:9-10
Romans 8:28-29
Ephesians 2:8-10
2 Corinthians 3:17-18, 4:6
Titus 2:11-14

Chapter 7

Mark 7:1-23
Colossians 2:20-23; 3:1-5, 16
Romans 12:2
Hebrews 3:12-13
Colossians 1:3, 9-12

Chapter 8

1 Corinthians 2:3-5, 1:18-25
2 Corinthians 10:10, 12:7-10, 4:7
Colossians 4:3-6, 3:16
Luke 6:45
Numbers 11:16-30
Acts 2:1-21, 4:23-31
Joel 2:28
1 Corinthians 12-14
Ephesians 4, 5:18-20
Romans 15:14-16
Philippians 1:3-18
Hebrews 3:7-15, 10:19-25
Matthew 28:16-20

Appendix 2

In the final chapter of this book, we summarized God's purpose for the world and for our lives. This is how we put it:

Because God's grand purpose for his creation is
- *to transfer forgiven rebels into his Son's kingdom*
- *and to transform them into his Son's image*

then his purpose for my life is that I should
- *die with Christ and rise to new life in his kingdom*
- *press forward to maturity in Christ by putting sin to death and putting on the character of Christ*
- *in love, help others move from wherever they are towards maturity in Christ by prayerfully speaking God's word to them.*

Our mission at Matthias Media is basically to produce resources of all kinds that equip Christians to pursue God's purpose in their lives—to grow to maturity in Christ, and to minister to others to see them grow to maturity in Christ as well.

Below are listed some of our most popular and useful resources that reinforce the ideas contained in this book, and provide training and encouragement to put them into practice. For more details about these resources and many others, visit our website: **matthiasmedia.com**

Resources to help you press forward to maturity in Christ

The Briefing

Matthias Media has been publishing *The Briefing* in various formats for more than two decades. It's now available as a free online web magazine, as well as a full-colour paper edition published six times a year in various formats and available by subscription. In *The Briefing* you'll find:

- Articles, audio and video to help Christians grow in their knowledge of God, and in their passion for godliness day by day.
- Ideas and examples to encourage all Christians in helping others grow towards maturity in Christ.
- A Christian perspective on the ideas and events of the world around us (including book reviews).
- Resources and ideas for pastors and other full-time gospel workers as they lead God's people in serving him.

For more information, visit the website: **matthiasmedia. com/briefing**

The Daily Reading Bible

The Daily Reading Bible is an all-in-one resource that helps you set your mind every day on God's word in the Bible.

Each volume contains around 60 undated readings. Each reading is designed to take around 15-20 minutes, and contains:

- the full text of the Bible passage for that reading
- some questions to get you thinking
- some 'points to ponder'
- some ideas to get you started in prayer.

It's all in one booklet that you can take with you anywhere—on the train, on the bus, to the park at lunchtime, or to your favourite armchair.

The short studies in this series are also available in the *XV* app for iPhone, iPad and iPod touch, along with an overview of the story of the Bible in 15 stages from creation through to new creation.

Guidebooks for Life

This is a series of straightforward, practical books that deal with the important nuts-and-bolts topics that Christians need to know about as we walk each day with our Master. Some Christian books are all theory and no practical application; others are all stories and tips with no substance. The Guidebooks for Life aim to achieve a vital balance—that is, to dig into the Bible and discover what God is telling us there, as well as apply that truth to our daily lives.

Key titles in the series include:

- *Encouragement: How words change lives* by Gordon Cheng
- *Guidance and the Voice of God* by Phillip Jensen and Tony Payne
- *A Sinner's Guide to Holiness* by John Chapman

The Trellis and the Vine by Colin Marshall and Tony Payne

All Christian ministry is a mixture of trellis and vine. There is vine work: the prayerful preaching and teaching of the word of God to see people converted and grow to maturity as disciples of Christ. Vine work is the Great Commission. And there is trellis work: creating and maintaining the physical and organizational structures and programs that support vine work and its growth.

The Trellis and the Vine helps you to take a look at the state of the trellis and the vine in your church, and answer the question of whether trellis work has taken over (as it has a habit of doing). Is the vine work being done by very few (perhaps only the pastor and only on Sundays)? And is the vine starting to wilt as a result?

This book digs into the Bible's view of Christian ministry, and looks at the kinds of changes we need to make if we are to fulfill the Great Commission of Christ, and see the vine flourish again.

Resources to help you move others forward to maturity in Christ

Towards the end of *The Thing Is* we looked at the following diagram, which helps us to visualize our goal of helping others move forward, step by step, towards maturity in Christ:

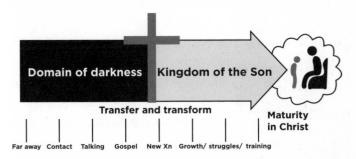

At Matthias Media, we divide all our resources into four categories that reflect this continuum of growth towards Christ:

- **Outreach**: talking about spiritual issues with our friends, and sharing the gospel with them
- **Follow-up**: establishing new and young Christians in the kingdom
- **Growth**: putting sin to death, and clothing ourselves with Christ's character
- **Training**: learning to serve others in **outreach**, **follow-up** and **growth**

Here are some of our key resources in each category.

Resources for outreach

Two Ways to Live by Phillip Jensen and Tony Payne

Two Ways to Live is a well-known memorable summary of the gospel that has been used to share the gospel with hundreds of thousands of people around the world. It comes in a range of styles, formats and languages, but each different resource that uses the *Two Ways to Live* framework features the same six-step logical presentation of what the Bible says about Jesus Christ. For more information, visit the website: **twowaystolive.com**

The Essential Jesus

This innovative 80-page book combines a fresh translation of Luke's Gospel with an introduction and conclusion based on the *Two Ways to Live* framework. The result is a very economical and effective way to share the gospel with lots of people.

Naked God by Martin Ayers

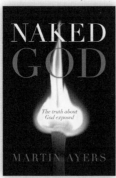

In *Naked God*, former lawyer Martin Ayers provides an opportunity for interested enquirers to examine the big questions: Is there a God? How can I know the truth given that different religions make different claims? And if there is a God, what real difference will he make to my life?

Resources for follow-up

Just for Starters

Used by thousands of churches worldwide, *Just for Starters* is widely regarded as *the* Bible study for following up new Christians. The seven studies look at what the Bible teaches on seven fundamental topics: Saved by God, Trusting in God, Living God's way, Listening to God, Talking to God, Meeting with God's family, Meeting the world.

There is a second set of studies in the series as well, called *Christian Living for Starters*.

Right Side Up by Paul Grimmond

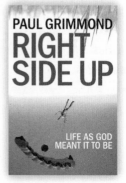

This book is especially designed for new Christians, to orient them to the new life they have embarked upon with Christ. It not only clearly explains the gospel (so that the foundations are solid), but also goes on to discuss the many practical issues and challenges that new believers face. It's a warm-hearted, engaging, exciting read about the adventure of the Christian life, and as such is very helpful as a refresher for longer-serving Christians as well.

Resources for growth

Bible studies

We have two main series of Bible studies:

- Pathway Bible Guides: short, simple Bible studies that are easy to digest
- Interactive Bible Studies: solid food for more established Christians.

Both series are designed mainly for small groups, although the Pathway series is also very suitable for one-to-one Bible study.

Although pitched at slightly different levels, both series focus closely on the passage of Scripture rather than bouncing too quickly into discussion or application; both seek to read the passage in its context; and both maintain a balance between providing input and direction, and allowing plenty of room for exploration and discovery.

Guidebooks for Life (with discussion guides)

Like many of our resources, the Guidebooks for Life series (described earlier) is not only excellent for seeking to grow ourselves; it is also an excellent tool for helping others grow. Get together with a friend (or in your home group) and decide to read through one of these helpful books together, using the supplied discussion guide to stimulate your conversation together.

Resources for training

The Course of Your Life by Tony Payne

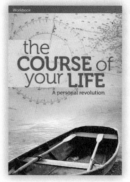

This course deals with many of the ideas in *The Thing Is* but in a way that a small group can work through and discuss over a few months. It also includes practical training on reading the Bible one-to-one with another person.

The course consists of seminars, one-to-one Bible reading sessions, video input (which the course leader can also choose to present personally using the notes in the leader's guide), and a special intensive during which course participants can take some time to think through the practical application of the ideas in the course.

For more information, visit the course website: **thecourseofyourlife.info**

One-to-one Bible Reading: A simple guide for every Christian by David Helm

This short, practical and very helpful book will train you in reading the Bible together with another person. It provides lots of useful ideas about how to start reading the Bible with someone (whether Christian or non-Christian), along with a large range of resources and methods for reading different parts of the Bible. This is a supremely useful little book.

Two Ways to Live training by Phillip Jensen and Tony Payne

Our best-known training program is *Two Ways to Live: Know and share the gospel*. This seven-session course teaches participants to know the gospel thoroughly for themselves, and then trains them in how to explain that message clearly and naturally in their own words, using the well-known *Two Ways to Live* framework. With role-plays, DVD and audio input, the course is easy to run and highly effective.

Six Steps courses

The other main plank in our training resources is the video-based *Six Steps* range, now with four titles in the series. Each one contains simple, straightforward training for every Christian in a basic area of Christian living and ministry:

- *Six Steps to Encouragement*: how to encourage one another with God's word
- *Six Steps to Talking About Jesus*: how to begin to share your faith with others
- *Six Steps to Reading your Bible*: how to dig into God's word for yourself
- *Six Steps to Loving Your Church*: how to love and build up others on Sunday

These courses are ideal for running in existing small groups as a framework for training people in knowledge, godliness and the ability to speak God's word to others for their growth in Christ.

Feedback on this resource

We really appreciate getting feedback about our resources—not just suggestions for how to improve them, but also positive feedback and ways they can be used. We especially love to hear that the resources may have helped someone in their Christian growth.

You can send feedback to us via the 'Feedback' menu in our online store, or write to us at info@matthiasmedia.com.au.

matthiasmedia

Matthias Media is an evangelical publishing ministry that seeks to persuade all Christians of the truth of God's purposes in Jesus Christ as revealed in the Bible, and equip them with high-quality resources, so that by the work of the Holy Spirit they will:

- abandon their lives to the honour and service of Christ in daily holiness and decision-making
- pray constantly in Christ's name for the fruitfulness and growth of his gospel
- speak the Bible's life-changing word whenever and however they can—in the home, in the world and in the fellowship of his people.

It was in 1988 that we first started pursuing this mission, and in God's kindness we now have more than 300 different ministry resources being used all over the world. These resources range from Bible studies and books through to training courses and audio sermons.

To find out more about our large range of very useful resources, and to access samples and free downloads, visit our website:

www.matthiasmedia.com

How to buy our resources

1. Direct from us over the internet:
   – in the US: www.matthiasmedia.com
   – in Australia and the rest of the world:
   www.matthiasmedia.com.au

2. Direct from us by phone:
   – in the US: 1 866 407 4530
   – in Australia: 1300 051 220
   – international: +61 2 9233 4627

> Register at our website for our **free** regular email update to receive information about the latest new resources **exclusive special offers**, and free articles to help you grow in your Christian life and ministry.

3. Through a range of outlets in various parts of the world. Visit **www.matthiasmedia.com/contact** for details about recommended retailers in your part of the world, including www.thegoodbook.co.uk in the United Kingdom.

4. Trade enquiries can be addressed to:
   – in the US and Canada: sales@matthiasmedia.com
   – in Australia and the rest of the world: sales@matthiasmedia.com.au

Preparing Just for Starters

Preparing Just for Starters is a self-paced training course with a difference. The workbook and the two accompanying audio CDs contain everything you need in order to learn how to use *Just for Starters*, a set of Bible studies that has been used for more than 30 years to follow-up new Christians and establish them in the basics of the faith. Setting your own schedule, you will be introduced to the *Just for Starters* studies and the part they can play in personal follow-up, and then you'll be led step-by-step through each of the seven studies.

Whether you have used *Just for Starters* before or are new to personal follow-up, this course will give you a deeper understanding of the Just for Starters studies, and greater confidence in using them.

One-to-One Bible Reading
A simple guide for every Christian
By David Helm

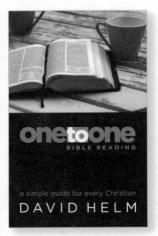

Can you think of people in your life that you would like to see progress spiritually—perhaps a non-Christian colleague, or a Christian friend at church, or a family member?

Imagine if you could help them understand more of God in a way that was simple and personal, and that didn't rely on getting them to a church program or event. Imagine if people could grow spiritually in a deeper, more meaningful way than an event, program or class could possibly achieve, guided on an individual basis by someone who cared for them personally.

What is this way? What is this activity that is so simple and so universal that it meets the discipleship needs of very different people at very different stages of discipleship, even non-Christians? We call it reading the Bible one-to-one. But what exactly is reading the Bible one-to-one? Why should we do it? Who is it for? And how do you do it in various contexts with different people?

In *One-to-One Bible Reading: a simple guide for every Christian*, David Helm answers these important questions.

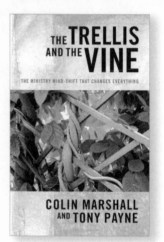